INTO THE WILD

Jon Krakauer

AUTHORED by Alice Cullina
UPDATED AND REVISED by Damien Chazelle

COVER DESIGN by Table XI Partners LLC
COVER PHOTO by Olivia Verma and © 2005 GradeSaver, LLC

BOOK DESIGN by Table XI Partners LLC

Published by GradeSaver LLC, www.gradesaver.com

First published in the United States of America by GradeSaver LLC. 2009

GRADESAVER, the GradeSaver logo and the phrase "Getting you the grade since 1999" are registered trademarks of GradeSaver, LLC

ISBN 978-1-60259-204-9

Printed in the United States of America

For other products and additional information please visit
http://www.gradesaver.com

Table of Contents

Table of Contents

Biography of Krakauer, Jon (1954-)

Jon Krakauer was born in 1954, the third of five children, and grew up in Corvallis, Oregon. His father, Lewis Krakauer, a doctor and weekend climber, introduced him to mountaineering when he was eight. He went to Hampshire College, from which he graduated in 1976, and then divided his time between Colorado, Alaska, and the Pacific Northwest, working as a carpenter and salmon fisherman, traveling around, and mountain climbing as much as possible.

Krakauer's father was greatly disappointed that Jon didn't go into medicine, but Jon was passionate about writing and climbing, and has accomplished many great mountain climbing feats. He has written for *Outside, Architectural Digest, The New York Times, The Washington Post*, and other publications, and in 1990 published two books: *Eiger Dreams*, a collection of mountaineering essays, and *Iceland: Land of the Sagas*, a book of his photographs.

In 1996 he reached the top of Mt. Everest, but four of his five teammates were killed in a storm as they descended from the peak. He wrote *Into Thin Air* about this calamity, and the general commercialization of Mt. Everest, and it became a #1 *New York Times* bestseller. The book has been translated into 24 languages, and has won numerous awards. *Into the Wild* was published in 1996, also to great acclaim and commercial success, and in 2003 Krakauer published [Under the Banner of Heaven: A Story of Violent Faith], which examines the nature of religious passion through the lens of Mormon Fundamentalism, a common religion in the area where he grew up. In September 2009, Krakauer's latest book, *Where Men Win Glory: The Odyssey of Pat Tillman*, about the football star turned army hero, was released.

About Into the Wild

In January 1993, Jon Krakauer published an article in *Outside* magazine about the death of Chris McCandless, a young Emory graduate who had donated all of his money to charity, gotten rid of all his belongings, changed his name, and, in April 1992, after two years of itinerant living, walked alone into the Alaskan wilderness with few supplies, intending to live off of the land. His body was found about four months later, in September 1992.

The article in *Outside* magazine garnered a great deal of attention, and Krakauer found himself obsessed with the question of what led McCandless to this extreme end. He also saw many parallels between McCandless's personality and behavior, and his own as a younger man. He thus decided to do significantly more research and to make a book out of the tale, and spent nearly three years researching the story in an effort to discover what exactly happened to McCandless.

Krakauer interviewed McCandless's family, friends, and as many of those as McCandless came across in his two years on the road as he could find. He also had access to McCandless's books and journals, all of his photos, and the letters he sent to people like Wayne Westerberg and Jan Burres. Using this information, as well as information about McCandless's childhood and time at college, Krakauer pieced together much of what drove McCandless to his rootless existence, and what he did during that time.

Into the Wild was the result of this research, and was published in 1996. The book, in trying to discover what exactly led McCandless to his mysterious end, and what happened once he was alone, also discusses Krakauer's own history, and the stories of many other famous or infamous figures who met their ends in the wilderness.

Into the Wild was published to great success, spending more than two years on the *New York* Times bestseller list. The book was also made into a movie in 2007. One of the questions Krakauer tried to answer in his research was what exactly had killed Chris McCandless. In the *Outside* magazine article, he posited that McCandless had mistaken the poisonous wild sweat pea for the nearly indistinguishable edible wild potato, and thus had inadvertently poisoned himself. This was what almost all journalists at the time also believed.

While continuing to research for the book, however, Krakauer found it hard to believe that McCandless had made that mistake, after successfully distinguishing between the two plants for weeks, and he decided that instead, the wild potato was poisonous, but only in the seeds. Analysis eventually showed this not to be true, however, and it was only long after the first edition of *Into the Wild* came out that Krakauer came up with his final theory--that McCandless's seeds had developed a poisonous mold when he stored them, and that that was what poisoned him.

Character List

Jon Krakauer

Jon Krakauer is the author and narrator of *Into the Wild*, whose life in certain ways parallels McCandless's. Obsessive about mountain climbing from his teens to his late twenties, like McCandless he also has issues with male authority figures, and has a very conflicted relationship with his father.

Christopher McCandless

Chris McCandless is the subject of *Into the Wild*. McCandless is an intelligent, extremely intense young man with a streak of stubborn idealism. He grows up in a wealthy suburb of Washington, D.C., where he succeeds both academically and athletically. He graduates from Emory University with honors in 1990, and soon afterwards gives all of his savings to charity, starts going by the name of "Alex," abandons almost all of his possessions, and spends two years hitchhiking and traveling around the west. He then hitchhikes to Alaska, where he walks alone into the wilderness north of Mt. McKinley in April 1992. He is found dead four months later.

Jim Gallien

Jim Gallien is a union electrician and accomplished hunter and woodsman who picks up "Alex" four miles outside of Fairbanks and drives him to Denali. He is the last person to see McCandless alive.

Ken Thompson

Ken Thompson is the owner of an Anchorage body shop who is with Gordon Samel and Ferdie Swanson on a hunting trip when they find McCandless's body.

Gordon Samel

Gordon Samel is an employee of Ken Thompson, and he is the one to find McCandless's body on what is supposed to be a moose hunting trip.

Ferdie Swanson

Ferdie Swanson is a construction worker and friend of Ken and Gordon who is with them when they find McCandless's body.

Butch Killian

Butch Killian is a coal miner and emergency medical technician from Healy, the closest town, who arrives at the bus soon after Samel has found McCandless's body.

Wayne Westerberg

Wayne Westerberg is the owner of a grain elevator in Carthage, South Dakota, who meets McCandless when he picks him up hitchhiking in 1990. He gives McCandless jobs multiple times, and becomes close to him.

Walt McCandless

Chris's father, Walt is an eminent aerospace engineer and the father of eight children from two marriages. He is fifty-six at the time of Chris's death. He is taciturn, passionate and stubborn, much like his son, and also brilliant, musically talented, with a mercurial temper.

Billie McCandless

Chris and Carine's mother, Billie is a very petite woman who meets Walt while working as a secretary at the company he works for before they split off to start their own company together. Like Walt and her children, she is very passionate, with a strong temper.

Carine McCandless

Carine is Chris's younger sister, with whom he is extremely close. Carine looks a lot like Chris, and is also energetic, self-assured, and a high-achiever, but unlike Chris is very gregarious, forgiving of people's faults, and happily fits into capitalist society.

Bud Walsh

Bud Walsh is a National Park Service ranger who finds McCandless's abandoned Datsun in the Mojave Desert.

Jan Burres

Jan Burres is a middle-aged rubber tramp who travels around the West selling knick-knacks at flea markets. She meets McCandless when she picks him up hitchhiking. They become close, and he stays in written contact with her until going into the Alaskan wilderness.

Peter Kalitka

Peter Kalitka is the private investigator hired by the McCandlesses to find Chris.

George Dreeszen

George Dreeszen is the talkative assistant manager at the McDonald's where McCandless works for a short period in Bullhead City.

Lori Zarza

Lori Zarza is the second assistant manager at the McDonald's where McCandless works in Bullhead City, who is surprised that Chris gets hired and encourages him to use better hygiene.

Charlie

Charlie is the somewhat crazy old man who gives McCandless a mobile home to live in temporarily while he is in Bullhead City.

Ronald Franz

Ronald Franz is an eighty-year old devout Christian and soldier who picks McCandless up hitchhiking and takes a strong liking to him. He has lost his wife and children long ago, and so feels a fatherly affection for Chris, whom he offers to adopt. After hearing of Chris's death, he stops believing in God.

Gail Borah

Gail Borah is Wayne Westerberg's longtime on-again, off-again girlfriend, a divorced mother of two who becomes close to McCandless while he is in Carthage.

Mary Westerberg

Mary Westerberg is Wayne Westerberg's mother, who has McCandless over for dinner, and hits it off with him immediately even though she doesn't usually like Westerberg's workers.

Gene Rosellini

Gene Rosellini is a brilliant man from a wealthy family who decides to see if he can live as primitive man did, and succeeds at it for over a decade before deciding his experiment has failed, and killing himself.

John Waterman

John Waterman is a very talented young climber from the suburbs of D.C., whose drive to climb dangerous slopes intensifies as he loses his mind, and who eventually embarks on a suicidal assent of Denali, and is never heard from again.

Carl McCunn

Carl McCunn is a thirty-five year old amateur photographer who hires a pilot to drop him in the wilderness for a five month long stay to take photographs of wildlife. He forgets to arrange for someone to pick him up, and so ends up killing himself once his rations run out.

Everett Ruess

Everett Ruess is a twenty year old born in 1914, who is intensely passionate about nature, and spends almost all of his time after he is sixteen on the move in a very similar manner to McCandless. He eventually disappears without a trace in Utah.

Ken Sleight

Ken Sleight is a sixty-five year old professional river guide who has closely studied the mystery of Ruess's disappearance, and has his own theory for what happened.

Sam McCandless

One of Chris's older half-brothers, Sam is the first to hear about Chris's death from the authorities.

Loren Johnson

McCandless's maternal grandfather, Loren is proud, stubborn, and dreamy, and never can quite fit into society, just like Chris. The two get along very well together. Loren is especially fond of wildlife, and finds hunting very emotionally difficult.

Gordy Cucullu

Gordy Cucullu is a younger member of the cross-country team of which McCandless is captain in high school.

Eric Hathaway

Eric Hathaway is a friend of McCandless's on his high school cross-country team.

Kris Maxie Gillmer

Kris Maxie Gillmer is a member of the girls' cross-country team at McCandless's high school, and one of Chris's closest friends at the school.

Chris Fish

Chris Fish is Carine's husband and partner in their auto-repair business.

Kai Sandburn

Kai Sandburn is a cheerful, outgoing woman who Krakauer meets on his quest to climb the Devil's Thumb.

Lewis Krakauer

Jon Krakauer's father, Lewis is a kind and generous man, but is extremely competitive and ambitious, and extends his aspirations to his five children. The only future he wants for Jon is for him to become a doctor, and Jon's rebellion against this leads to a wide chasm between the two of them. Lewis ends up losing his mind due to misguided self-medication for a painful medical condition.

Gaylord Stuckey

Gaylord Stuckey is a sixty-three year old man who meets McCandless in the Laird River Hotsprings, and, taking a liking to him, drives him the rest of the way to Fairbanks.

Roman Dial

An Alaskan companion who accompanies Krakauer to McCandless's bus, Roman grew up in and felt stifled by the same suburbs as McCandless, and makes Alaska his home immediately after graduating high school at sixteen. He teaches at Alaska Pacific University and is known throughout Alaska for many brave back-country feats.

Dan Solie

Dan Solie is another Alaskan companion who accompanies Krakauer to McCandless's bus.

Andrew Liske

Andrew Liske is a friend of Roman Dial's from California who also accompanies Krakauer to McCandless's bus.

Sir John Franklin

Sir John Franklin is a nineteenth century British naval officer whose ignorance and hubris leads to the death of around one hundred and forty men entrusted to his leadership on Arctic expeditions.

Major Themes

The Allure of the Wilderness

To McCandless and many others of his ilk, the wilderness has a very specific allure. McCandless sees the wilderness as a purer state, a place free of the evils of modern society, where someone like him can find out what he is really made of, live by his own rules, and be completely free. And this is not just naïveté; McCandless's journal entries show that he does find some answers, some keys to living the way he wants to live.

Yet, it is also true that the reality of day-to-day living in the wilderness is not as romantic as he and others like him imagine it to be. McCandless spends so much time trying to find food to keep himself alive that he has little time to consciously appreciate the wilderness, as is evidenced by the fact that his journal consists almost solely of lists of the food that he finds and eats every day. Perhaps this explains why many of his heroes who wrote about the wilderness, for example, Jack London, never actually spent much time living in it.

Forgiveness

Forgiveness, and the danger inherent in the inability to forgive, are central themes in *Into the Wild*. Chris McCandless is shown to be a very compassionate person, who is unwilling to ignore the fact that so many people are starving or hungry around him, and feels a personal responsibility to help them. Yet his actions are ultimately selfish, and do great harm to those who love him most. Moreover, his inability to forgive his parents' mistakes seems to be at the center of this seeming contradiction between his compassionate nature and his sometimes cruel behavior.

There is certainly more behind his odyssey than just anger at his parents, but his resentment of them does spread into the rest of his life, and seems to be closely connected to how isolated he becomes at Emory. This, in turn, adds to his revulsion against society generally, which is clearly a driving factor in his deciding to go into the wilderness. One is left to wonder if, had McCandless found a way to forgive his parents for their shortcomings, he would not have felt the need to go to such extreme lengths in his quest for answers.

Ultimate Freedom

McCandless describes what he is looking for on his odyssey, particularly on the Alaska trip, as "ultimate freedom." It would seem that this largely represents, to him, freedom from other people's rules and authority over him. Throughout his whole life he finds authority particularly oppressive, especially when exercised by anyone who he feels only has such power over him for arbitrary reasons. To live completely alone, in a world where the only laws he feels the need to follow are those of nature, is to him ultimate freedom.

Yet this level of freedom requires total isolation, for to be with others means to have obligations to them. Thus, McCandless's quest for freedom becomes, also, a refutation of any and all intimacy with others. This kind of freedom is inherently selfish. By living only according to his own rules and those of nature, no matter how principled and deeply-thought, McCandless is implicitly living only for his own best interest. For example, he refuses to get a hunting license because he doesn't think it is any of the government's business what he eats; were everyone to act this way, animal populations would be destroyed, and food supplies threatened. McCandless's ultimate freedom is thus limited in scope, for on any larger scale it would be dangerous and potentially disastrous.

The Allure of Danger

The allure of danger and high-risk activities is central to *Into the Wild*. Krakauer does not believe that this allure is significant to everyone, but it certainly is to a specific kind of young man -- one who is intense, passionate, driven and ambitious, but not satisfied with the opportunities or challenges society presents to him. These young men also always seem to have some kind of demon driving them, whether it is a troubled relationship with their fathers, as with McCandless, Krakauer, and John Waterman, or something else.

For Krakauer, at least, the risk in his activities brought him to a point of meditation—because he is often only one mistake away from death, he has to focus utterly, and this allows him to escape from those problems that would otherwise eat away at him. There is also the thrill of pure accomplishment, man against only nature and himself, which allows him to feel that he truly knows what he is capable of, that he doesn't need to rely on others, or on society, to survive.

Valuing Principles over People

One of the primary qualities McCandless constantly exhibited, which in turn led many to respect him, was his adherence to principles. He does not simply preach that his parents are too materialistic, or state that he won't be as greedy as he believes them to be. Instead, he lives by his anti-materialism completely, giving away all of his life savings to charity, only making the bare minimum of money that he needs to survive, and keeping as few possessions as he possibly can.

While this adherence to principle is admirable and, unfortunately, unusual, McCandless does seem to put his principles above people, which leads him to cause hurt without really intending to do so. For example, in college Chris decides that he has a moral problem with gifts, and so will no longer accept or give them. Although this decision is based on a sense of morality, it in fact causes McCandless to hurt those who care about him. This may be related to his intimacy problems, for as long as he doesn't let people get too close, he won't be put in a position of having to choose them over his principles.

The Elusiveness of Identity

The elusiveness of identity, or of truly understanding someone's identity, is a theme both explicitly and implicitly present throughout *Into the Wild*. Krakauer spends about three years putting together first the article on Chris McCandless, and then this book. He talks to almost anyone who met McCandless, even fleetingly. He follows McCandless's trails, reads his journals, even reads the articles he wrote for the student paper at Emory. Krakauer also feels he has an extra level of understanding, because he was much like Chris when he was in his twenties.

Yet even with all of this, at the end of the book, Krakauer acknowledges that McCandless's presence remains elusive. As closely as he may have studied him, as well as he has come to "know" him, there are a few fundamental questions which no one, not even Chris's parents, can find a satisfactory answer to. Most important of these is how someone so compassionate, kind, and intelligent could have ended up devastating his parents, and all of those who loved him, so profoundly. The ultimate inability to truly know another person is thus at the heart of *Into the Wild*.

The Father-Son Relationship

The father-son relationship, and the potential for dysfunction within it, is an important theme in *Into the Wild*. Both Krakauer and McCandless are highly ambitious, and have highly ambitious fathers. The problem arises in that their fathers' ambitions for them are very different from their own, and their strong wills and passion for their own kind of ambition—in Krakauer's case, mountain climbing, and in McCandless's, the wilderness and anti-materialist living—cause great rifts between father and son.

For both McCandless and Krakauer, the combination of trying to please a difficult-to-please father, resenting authority, and discovering their fathers' own great failings leads to an almost insurmountable rift. Krakauer was able to forgive his father only once he was no longer the same man. McCandless died before he had the opportunity to grow out of his anger.

Glossary of Terms

amalgam
mixture

anachronistic
not appropriate to the times

canted
sloping

carapace
an animal's shell

contumacious
resistant to authority; flagrantly disobedient or rebellious

coppice
a grove of small trees

denuded
stripped by erosion

dunning
darkly bleak and depressing

eremitic
like a hermit

escarpments
steep ridges or cliffs forming the boundary of a plateau area

garrulous
very talkative

hyperkinetic
unusually active, mobile

itinerant
traveling from place to place

leather tramps

vagabonds without a vehicle, who thus have to hitchhike or walk

lenity

the quality of being or acting lenient

mawkish

sentimental in a contrived way

morass

an area of soggy ground; a situation that impedes or prevents progress, that is hard to get through

muskeg

an area of swamp or boggy land covered in moss, leaves and dead plant matter

opprobrium

scorn or criticism

pellucid

transparent

plebeian

common or coarse

ramparts

fortified embankments

rictus

a strange grin or grimace

rubber tramps

vagabonds who have a vehicle

saguaro

a large cactus found in the American Southwest that can grow to be sixty feet tall

scudding

sailing with a strong wind blowing from behind

sere

dry and withered

sonorous
with loud, deep, and clear tones

stasis
a state without motion or development

taiga
subarctic coniferous forests

turgid
pompous and overcomplicated

Short Summary

Into the Wild is the true story of Chris McCandless, a young Emory graduate who is found dead in the Alaskan wilderness in September 1992, when he is twenty-four. McCandless grows up in wealthy Virginia suburbs of Washington, D.C., and is a very gifted athlete and scholar, who from an early age shows deep intensity, passion, and a strict moral compass. After graduating from high school McCandless spends the summer alone on a road trip across the country, during which he discovers that his father secretly had a second family during Chris's childhood. McCandless returns home and starts as a freshman at Emory, but his anger over this betrayal and his parents' keeping it from him grows worse over time.

By the time that McCandless is a senior at Emory, he lives monastically, has driven away most of his friends with his intensity and moral certitude, and barely keeps in touch with his parents. He lets his parents think that he is interested in law school, but instead, after graduating with honors, he donates his $25,000 savings anonymously to charity, gets in his car, and drives away without telling anyone where he is going, abandoning the use of his real name along the way. He never contacts his parents or sister, Carine, again.

Not too long after leaving Atlanta, McCandless deserts his car in the desert after a flash flood wets the engine, and from then on, he hitchhikes around the Northwest, getting jobs here and there but not staying anywhere for long, often living on the streets, and keeping as little money and as few possessions as he can. During this time he gets to know a few people rather closely, and everyone admires his intensity and willingness to live completely by his beliefs, but he avoids true intimacy.

After about two years of itinerant travel, McCandless settles on a plan to go to Alaska and truly live in the wilderness, completely alone, and with very few supplies, to see if he can do it, to push himself to the very extremes. He spends a few months preparing, learning all he can about hunting, edible plants, etc, and then he leaves South Dakota, where he'd been working, and hitchhikes to Fairbanks. Those whom he tells about the plan all warn him that he needs to be better prepared, or should wait until later in the spring, but he is adamant and stubborn.

In April of 1992 McCandless gets dropped off near Mt. McKinley, and hikes into the wilderness. He spends the next sixteen weeks hunting small game, foraging, reading, and living in a deserted bus made to be a shelter for hunters, not seeing a single human the entire time. He is successful for the most part, although he loses significant weight. In late July, however, McCandless probably eats some moldy seeds, and the mold contains a poison that essentially causes him to starve to death, no matter how much he eats, and he is too weak to gather food anyway. McCandless is quickly incapacitated by the poison. Realizing he is going to die, he writes a goodbye message, and a few weeks later some hunters find his body in the bus.

Quotes and Analysis

"McCandless was thrilled to be on his way north, and he was relieved as well—relieved that he had again evaded the impending threat of human intimacy, of friendship, and all the messy emotional baggage that comes with it. He had fled the claustrophobic confines of his family. He'd successfully kept Jan Burres and Wayne Westerberg at arm's length, flitting out of their lives before anything was expected of him. And now he'd slipped painlessly out of Ron Franz's life as well."

Into the Wild, 55

This passage illuminates McCandless's deep problems with intimacy, which are very central in his ultimately fatal two-year quest for meaning and peace. During these two years, McCandless doesn't contact his sister, with whom he was very close, and while he meets many people and becomes close to a few, he always makes sure to maintain a certain distance.

In this passage, he is just leaving Ron Franz, who spends the next year or so waiting for his return, living by his tenets, while McCandless ignores the responsibilities and bonds of intimacy by going into the wilderness, where he only has himself to account to. In allowing himself to forget about the responsibilities one has in any close relationships, he ignores the harm done to those who love him when he risks his safety and his life.

"Please return all mail I receive to the sender. It might be a very long time before I return South. If this adventure proves fatal and you don't ever hear from me again, I want you to know you're a great man. I now walk into the wild."

Into the Wild, 69

This passage consists of McCandless's own words, written on his last postcard to Wayne Westerberg before he goes into the Alaskan wilderness. The fact that he acknowledges the chance that he might not survive has been used as evidence that his trek was suicidal in intent, but this seems highly unlikely. Instead, this acknowledgment of the risk, and of what is truly at stake, shows that his arrogance and hubris are not as extreme as many imagine—he does not want to die, but he knows very well that he is embarking on a dangerous adventure, and that his margin for error is very slight. He feels this is worth it, however, for the real experience of living completely independently and freely, and his excitement can be seen in the final, terse sentence of his postcard to Westerberg.

"A trancelike state settles over your efforts; the climb becomes a clear-eyed dream. Hours slide by like minutes. The accumulated clutter of day-to-day existence—the lapses of conscience, the unpaid bills, the bungled opportunities, the dust under the couch, the inescapable prison of your genes—all of it is temporarily forgotten, crowded from your thoughts by an overpowering clarity of purpose and by the seriousness of the task at hand."

Into the Wild, 142-143

This passage describes Krakauer's feelings while climbing the Devils Thumb, and is, essentially, his explanation of the allure of mountain climbing, or of high-risk activities in general. It becomes clear, here, that it serves as a kind of escapism, for him at least. The intense focus required to survive such activities means that the mundane problems of daily life cannot intrude, and Krakauer can reach a kind of meditative state.

McCandless's treks are also clearly escapism on some level. He seems to be trying to escape from the responsibilities and bonds of human relationships; by going into the wild, alone, with no way to contact the outside world, and by having to focus his full attention on keeping himself alive, he cannot be called on to participate in relationships with those who care most about him.

"Seven weeks after the body of his son turned up in Alaska wrapped in a blue sleeping bag that Billie had sewn for Chris from a kit, Walt studies a sailboat scudding beneath the window of his waterfront townhouse. 'How is it,' he wonders aloud as he gazes blankly across Chesapeake Bay, 'that a kid with so much compassion could cause his parents so much pain?'"

Into the Wild, 103-104

This passage is emblematic of the problem at the core of McCandless's story. From what Krakauer learns about him, he seems to have been a deeply compassionate person, and a significant part of his two-year quest was fueled by his sense of injustice at how selfishly and greedily most Americans lived. His risky behavior over this time is, however, deeply selfish, in that it causes pain to all those who love him, and especially his family, who for two years do not even know if he is alive. And indeed, this is not just a side effect of his quest, but part of its aim—he explicitly wanted to cut his parents out of his life, and his anger at them seems to have been a large part of the source of his need to be always on the move. And thus the question that Walt McCandless poses in this passage, and which Krakauer tries to find an answer to throughout the book—how could such a caring, compassionate person act so selfishly?

"It is easy, when you are young, to believe that what you desire is no less than what you deserve, to assume that if you want something badly enough, it is your God-given right to have it. When I decided to go to Alaska that April, like Chris McCandless, I was a raw youth who mistook passion for insight and acted according to an obscure, gap-ridden logic. I thought climbing the Devils Thumb would fix all that was wrong with my life. In the end, of course, it changed almost nothing. But I came to appreciate that mountains make poor receptacles for dreams. And I lived to tell my tale."

Into the Wild, 155

This passage is illustrative of Krakauer's feelings about McCandless. He does not think McCandless is so naïve or arrogant as many, especially in Alaska, do, but he does see that he was young, and had many of the common misperceptions of the young, and claims that that was really his main flaw. The implication of this passage is that, had McCandless survived, he likely would have ended up maturing—learning to be close to people, to forgive flaws in those he loved, to interact with society and the world in less extreme ways. Because he dies, however—which is certainly not any more deserved than if Krakauer had on Devils Thumb—he will never have that opportunity, and instead is blamed for his ignorance and hubris.

"Two years he walks the earth, no phone, no pool, no pets, no cigarettes. Ultimate freedom. An extremist. An aesthetic voyager whose home is the road. Escaped from Atlanta. Thou shalt not return, 'cause "the West is the best." And now after two rambling years comes the final and greatest adventure, the climactic battle to kill the false being within and victoriously conclude the spiritual revolution. Ten days and nights of freight trains and hitchhiking bring him to the great white North. No longer to be poisoned by civilization he flees, and walks alone upon the land to become lost in the wild. – Alexander Supertramp, May 1992."

Into the Wild, 163

This passage shows how McCandless feels about his journey so far, right after he walks into the wilderness. He is clearly proud of himself, and proud of what he has accomplished, and deeply excited for the Alaskan "greatest adventure." It also shows, however, that he probably intends to rejoin civilization, even though he describes it as poisonous, for he calls this his "final" adventure, which will "conclude the spiritual revolution."

And though he writes "Thou shalt not return", the implication is not that he is walking into the wilderness to die, but that he will not go back to the East (since over his two-year journey he has fallen deeply in love with the American West). Finally, the passage shows how intertwined his need for independence and freedom is with his inability to let people too close, as he likens his entrance into the wilderness to fleeing and emphasizes that he is alone, and that only now can he enjoy "Ultimate freedom."

"As she studies the pictures, she breaks down from time to time, weeping as only a mother who has outlived a child can weep, betraying a sense of loss so huge and irreparable that the mind balks at taking its measure. Such bereavement, witnessed at close range, makes even the most eloquent apologia for high-risk activities ring fatuous and hollow."

Into the Wild, 132

This passage, about Billie McCandless after Chris's death, emphasizes that no matter how well-intentioned Chris may have been, his behavior was deeply cruel to his parents and family. The passage is also interesting because of the meta-commentary it offers. Over the course of the book, Krakauer's view of McCandless is largely forgiving, and Krakauer certainly understands the allure that high-risk activities held for him. Yet here he acknowledges that in the face of a parent's devastation from the loss of a son, it is very difficult to defend McCandless's behavior, no matter how well-intentioned or important it seemed to him at the time, thus implying that *Into the Wild* itself cannot defend McCandless when it comes to the pain his parents suffer.

"Roman, Andrew, and I stay up well past midnight, trying to make sense of McCandless's life and death, yet his essence remains slippery, vague, elusive."

Into the Wild, 186

This sentence is representative of one of the significant themes of the book—that it is impossible to ever really know another person's story, what drives them, how they end up where they do, etc., and that this is a problem inherent in biography. It looms even larger over this specific biography because McCandless has died, and has left a fairly elusive trail. His journals are largely only descriptions of events and foods, and there spans almost a whole year during which he doesn't leave any documentation. Krakauer does all he can to "make sense of McCandless's life and death," and he ultimately seems to come very close; yet a true, full understanding remains impossible.

"'I guess I just can't help identifying with the guy,' Roman allows as he pokes the coals with a stick. 'I hate to admit it, but not so many years ago it could easily have been me in the same kind of predicament. When I first started coming to Alaska, I think I was probably a lot like McCandless: just as green, just as eager. And I'm sure there are plenty of other Alaskans who had a lot in common with McCandless when they first got here, too, including many of his critics. Which is maybe why

they're so hard on him. Maybe McCandless reminds them a little too much of their former selves.'"

Into the Wild, 186

This passage again emphasizes that it was McCandless's death—caused by an innocent mistake though it might have been—that has made so many Alaskans look down upon him. Krakauer's friend Roman is famous for having accomplished a similarly dangerous and perhaps somewhat misguided feat, but had he died he would have likely been seen as McCandless now is. And Roman makes the point that this anger is probably because he is not the only one who sees himself in McCandless. By reminding people who either have or who used to have similar tendencies just how much is at stake when they indulge in risky behavior, McCandless essentially is a reminder of their own mortality.

"It is hardly unusual for a young man to be drawn to a pursuit considered reckless by his elders; engaging in risky behavior is a rite of passage in our culture no less than in most others. Danger has always held a certain allure. That, in large part, is why so many teenagers drive too fast and drink too much and take too many drugs, why it has always been so easy for nations to recruit young men to go to war. It can be argued that youthful derring-do is in fact evolutionarily adaptive, a behavior encoded in our genes. McCandless, in his fashion, merely took risk-taking to its logical extreme."

182

This passage underscores that McCandless's behavior is not completely unique or unusual. Though he obviously lives in a way that very few do, and particularly very few who grow up with the opportunities he has, the driving force behind his behavior is not unusual. This also reflects the idea that, had he survived, he would have been looked upon with admiration, likely, and would have been considered a person who had accomplished something impressive. Because he died, however, many have vilified him, and have seen in his daring only arrogance and stupidity, when in reality it was probably mostly influenced by his youth.

Summary and Analysis of Chapters 1-3

Jim Gallien sees a young man hitchhiking four miles outside of Fairbanks, and he picks him up. The hitchhiker introduces himself as Alex. Alex tells Jim that he is heading to Denali, where he plans to hike into the wilderness and live off of the land for a few months. Jim is concerned, because he notices that Alex's pack seems awfully light and he lacks a lot of essential tools, especially for the season, but he is at least a little reassured by Alex's sane demeanor and intelligent questions.

Alex tells Jim that he plans to go to the end of a little known path that peters out into the wilderness north of Mt. McKinley. Jim does his best to dissuade Alex—the hunting isn't good there, the grizzlies are fierce—but Alex won't budge. He even offers to take Alex to Anchorage to buy him some better gear, but Alex says he'll be fine with what he has. He also tells Jim that he doesn't have a hunting license, and no one knows where he is going—he hasn't spoken to anyone in his family for nearly two years. Jim convinces Alex to take his boots and some sandwiches his wife made for him, then he takes a picture for Alex at the trail head and leaves him there on April 28, 1992.

McCandless follows a trail called the Stampede Trail, which was blazed in the 1930s by a legendary Alaska miner. In 1961, Yukon Construction started to upgrade the trail, but gave up in 1963, leaving a bus outfitted to house workers along the trail as a shelter for hunters and trappers (although it is rarely used). In early September 1992, three moose hunters, Ken Thompson, Gordon Samel and Ferdie Swanson, go out to the bus, where they find a couple from Anchorage standing about fifty feet away, looking disturbed.

A powerful smell is coming from the bus, and there is a note taped to it written by Chris McCandless, saying that he is injured, weak, near death, and in need of assistance. The couple is too disturbed to look inside the bus, so Samel looks through the window, and sees a sleeping bag that might have something inside it. He goes around the other way, and sees a head protruding from it. McCandless has been dead for two weeks when they find him.

Samel thinks the body should be evacuated immediately, but Butch Killian, another hunter who soon after comes upon the scene, is the only one whose vehicle is large enough, and he thinks it should be left to the state troopers, so he drives back until he can get a signal to radio them the information. The police helicopter comes the next morning, and they examine the scene before taking McCandless's body, note, diary, camera and film back to Anchorage.

For the autopsy, McCandless's remains prove too badly decomposed for much to be clear, but as there is no evidence of massive internal injury or broken bones, starvation is posited as the most likely cause of death. McCandless was carrying no identification, so although there are pictures of him from his camera, and his name signed at the bottom of the SOS note he wrote, the police do not know where he is from or how to get in touch with his family.

We flash back to earlier. Wayne Westerberg, the owner of a grain elevator in Carthage, South Dakota, meets McCandless when he picks him up hitchhiking. McCandless ends up staying in his trailer for a few days, and Westerberg tells him to look him up if he ever needs work. McCandless comes back a few weeks later and starts working for Westerberg. He is one of the hardest workers Westerberg has ever seen, willing to do even the most unpleasant jobs, and finishing everything he starts. McCandless lives in a house owned by Westerberg with some of his other employees, which he really enjoys.

Westerberg, however, has to serve some time not too long after McCandless's arrival, and so although McCandless has found a lot to love in the town, there is no work for him without Westerberg, and he moves on. He keeps in touch with Westerberg from then until he goes into the wilderness, and tells almost everyone he meets that he is from South Dakota.

McCandless is actually from Annandale, Virginia, a wealthy suburb of Washington, D.C., where he grew up living with his father, Walt, an aerospace engineer, mother Billie, and younger sister Carine. In May 1990 (we have again flashed back further in the past), Chris graduates from Emory. His parents believe that he is planning on law school. The day after, which happens to be Mother's Day, Chris gives Billie a gift and sentimental card, which is extremely touching because for the past two years he has refused to give or accept gifts on principle. Not too long before that, for example, Chris became very angry when they offered to buy him a new car as a graduation gift, or to help him pay for law school.

After graduation Chris tells them that he is intending to spend the summer traveling, and then a few weeks later he writes them a note with his final transcript, which will be the last communication he ever offers to his family. When they go to stop by his apartment in August—he doesn't have a phone—they find that he moved out at the end of June without telling them. Five weeks earlier he had packed up all of his belongings and driven off in his beloved old Datsun, changing his name to Alex Supertramp to symbolically complete cutting himself off from his past.

Analysis

In *Into the Wild*, it quickly becomes very clear that Chris McCandless's story elicits strong reactions from people. In Krakauer's opening note, he explains that the original story he wrote for *Outside* magazine prompted more letters of response from readers than any other article ever in the magazine. Many of these reactions are strongly negative, but it is also clear that Krakauer, and almost everyone who met Chris, find something very admirable in him and in his story, or at least parts of it. This opening note also makes clear what the book's primary focus will be—not suspense or adventure, as Krakauer has already told us the ending, but instead the investigation of what drove McCandless, who he was, and how his life came to end so tragically.

In these opening chapters, Krakauer shows us many people who get along well with McCandless, and who have strongly positive things to say about him, even if they only spent a few hours driving him somewhere. Often, these people doubt him at first, assuming, based on his looks, hygiene, or Alaskan plans that he is foolish, uneducated, or some equivalent, but he is able to change people's minds about him very quickly. Thus, according to Krakauer's characterization, although McCandless certainly is flawed, and makes some mistakes that end in his death, the common belief that he is naïve and arrogant is shown to be, if not completely wrong, at least an unfair oversimplification.

McCandless has a few key characteristics that often change people's minds about him quickly. He is obviously intelligent and well-educated, and his passion for and intensity regarding his lifestyle and his forthcoming Alaska trip make it clear that he is not just following a whim. He is also incredibly hard-working, and even when he is not the most skilled, he proves himself a valuable employee to whoever hires him, willing to do any task, no matter how unpleasant or menial. His insistence on living by his beliefs and morals makes him stand out even more.

McCandless is, however, also very stubborn, as it quickly becomes clear in these opening chapters. Although he always pushes himself to work very hard and do the best job he can, he does not respond well to any criticism, or to any exhibition of authority at all. His stubbornness leads him to refuse any help from Jim Gallien, who goes so far as to offer to drive him far out of his way to buy him better equipment for his Alaskan trip. It also leads him to ignore any advice he gets, even from those with much more experience, if it would mean he would have to alter his Alaskan plans at all.

This stubbornness is closely related to what seems to be McCandless's most devastating flaw: his selfishness. He is passionately insistent on his own ability to take care of himself, on his right to freedom, from government law, from the responsibilities of intimacy, from the bounds of safety. This, though not selfish at heart, translates into selfishness as McCandless hurts those who love him most in his quest for total freedom. Though he is admirably trying to live as best he can by his own beliefs and morals, he doesn't pause to reflect on how his actions are painful to those around him, and this ultimately leads to his death.

The fact that the reader knows this will be the end from the beginning creates many moments of dramatic irony. The most profound example in this section is when Jim Gallien offers McCandless different kinds of help, and McCandless insists that he will be fine. The reader of course knows that this will absolutely not be the case. This moment is also an early example of one of the book's motifs—that of moments where Krakauer shows a decision or twist of fate that leads McCandless to his death, moments could have easily gone the other way instead. Another example in this section is Wayne Westerberg's prison sentence, without which Krakauer implies McCandless may very well have stayed happily and safely in Carthage.

Summary and Analysis of Chapters 4-5

In October 1990, McCandless's Datsun is found abandoned in the Mojave Desert by Bud Walsh, a National Park Service ranger. McCandless had driven it to the Lake Mead National Recreation Area in July, and against posted regulations, had driven it off road in the park and had pitched a campsite. A few days later, flash flooding almost washed away his campsite, and his car's engine got so wet he couldn't get it to start.

Because he wasn't supposed to have driven off-road, he couldn't get help from the rangers, and so he left the car with a note saying whoever can get the car to work can keep it. He uses this as another impetus to rid himself of unnecessary baggage, burning his money and leaving all of almost his belongings with the car. After being found by Bob Walsh, it ends up being used by the Park Service for undercover drug enforcement work. McCandless spends the next few months hitchhiking around the West, allowing his life to be shaped by circumstance, sharing the company of other vagabonds, having minor run-ins with the law.

In Oregon, a pair of rubber tramps spots McCandless picking berries by the side of the road, and he ends up camping with them for a week or so before continuing North up the coast. When McCandless gets a ticket for hitchhiking, he gives the officer his parents' address in Annandale, and so they soon after receive the ticket, which they give to a private investigator, Peter Kalitka, for him to use as a starting off point to find Chris. He follows many leads, but nothing comes up until he discovers that Chris donated his entire life savings to OXFAM, a charity that fights hunger.

After leaving Westerberg's place in South Dakota, McCandless heads south. In Arizona he buys a canoe on impulse, deciding to row down the Colorado River to the Gulf of California. He makes his way south, sending a postcard to Westerberg on the way, and sneaks through the border with Mexico. Once there, though, the river splits up into lots of small and confusing canals, and he has trouble finding his way.

Eventually he comes upon some duck hunters who speak English, who tell him there is no waterway to the sea, but who offer to tow his canoe to the ocean for him. Upon reaching his destination, he slows down his pace and takes his time camping and paddling along the coast. On January 11, 1991, he is almost carried out to sea in a bad storm, and after managing to survive decides to abandon the canoe and return back north.

He is caught by immigration authorities trying to slip back through the border without identification, but manages to convince them to let him go, although they keep his gun. He spends the next six weeks moving around the Southwest, and at one point goes to LA to get a job and an ID, but finds he can't handle society, and leaves again immediately. Not too long after he gets a job in an Italian restaurant in Las

Vegas, living on the streets, but he only lasts for a few months before he hits the road again.

After leaving Las Vegas, McCandless stops keeping a journal for the next year, nor does he have a working camera at this time, so little is known about how he spends the year. He spends July and August on the Oregon coast, then goes south again and east into the desert, ending up in Bullhead City, Arizona in early October. Although the town is essentially a collection of strip malls, McCandless takes a strong liking to it and settles there for a few months, probably longer than anywhere between leaving Atlanta and ending up in Alaska.

In Bullhead City he works at McDonald's, and even goes so far as to open a savings account, and uses his real name and social security number for the job, uncharacteristically. His coworkers don't get to know him very well, although they remember him as dependable, but off in his own world. Lori Zarza, the second assistant manager, is delegated to tell him that he needs to have somewhat better hygiene, and not long after this he quits.

During this time McCandless tries to hide from his coworkers the fact that he was homeless, camping outside of town and living in a semi-deserted mobile home shown to him by Charlie, who McCandless meets in a restroom, and finds to be rather crazy. Charlie remembers McCandless as a nice guy, but a little strange and intense, and remembers him always talking about Alaska. He leaves Bullhead City and goes to visit Jan Burress and Bob at the Niland Slabs.

While there, McCandless helps Jan man her table at the flea market, helping organize and sell books, and especially pushing Jack London. He also talks continually about the trip to Alaska he is planning, asking Bob for survival advice and doing calisthenics to try and get himself in shape. When he says he has to move on, Jan tries to give him some money and some long underwear, but he refuses to take anything.

Analysis

This section makes McCandless's intense distaste for society abundantly clear. In these chapters, he comes close to rejoining society a few times, going to Los Angeles with the intention of getting a new ID and possibly a job, working in Las Vegas, staying in Bullhead City longer than he has stayed anywhere else, and even working for a McDonald's using his real name and social security number. Yet each time, he finds himself quickly moving on again, unable or unwilling to reintegrate himself. His use of his social security number for the McDonald's job highlights the fact that Peter Kalitka, his parents' private investigator, as a character symbolizes the motif of moments that McCandless is almost saved. Kalitka finds clues, but he never finds the most important ones, ones that could actually lead he and Billie and Walt to Chris, and to potentially saving him.

In Los Angeles, he is barely able to venture into the city before he becomes too disgusted by the idea of rejoining society. He only lasts for a few weeks in Vegas, and though he stays in Bullhead City for an unusually long period of time, it is not really a city but a collection of strip malls, and he is there on the margins, camping out and squatting. He can't integrate into the culture at the McDonald's where he works because he is unwilling to improve his hygiene when asked, and thus his foray into "society" is ultimately short-lived.

This distaste for society seems closely related to his distaste for authority. Although he expounds on the hypocrisy of materialism, the cruelty of letting people starve while others do well, it never seems to actually be these issues that push him out of society again, but instead it is someone telling him what to do, or trying to impose their rules on him or control him in any way, that leads to his departure. Even from those he likes and respects, he often resents any advice or attempts to curtail his desires, as when he starts to talk about the Alaska trip. This stubbornness about accepting help is all the more emphasized because of the dramatic irony inherent in McCandless's insistence that he will be fine, that he can take care of himself, as in the first section with Jim Gallien, and in this section with Jan Burres.

In this section we also start to see clearly just how rare McCandless's passion is, and how deeply influenced by literature. Tolstoy and Jack London are two of his favorite authors, whom he pushes on whoever he thinks has the right mindset for them, and whose philosophies and morals he tries to live by. He doesn't seem to think or care about, however, the fact that neither of these two figures truly lived the lives they espoused, and London especially was never much of an outdoorsman at all. This both emphasizes McCandless's ability to ignore that which would negatively affect his theories, but also how passionate he truly was, for he did not just want to share these beliefs, but to, unusually, truly live by them.

This also highlights the importance of perspective to this story. McCandless is able to ignore the worst things about his favorite authors, because he finds their ideals and philosophies so enticing, but this act of ignoring means his perspective is limited. The awareness of perspective is essential in a book about someone living on the margins of society, in a way that many people think reflects a mental illness. In this section, the idea of differing perspective is symbolized in Charlie, who McCandless refers to as crazy, but who himself calls McCandless strange.

This insistence on following things through, on living the way you think is best, can also be seen in McCandless's Mexico trip. He decides, completely on a whim when he comes upon a used canoe, that he will canoe down the Colorado River, through Mexico to the Gulf of California. When this becomes much more difficult than expected—in Mexico, the Colorado branches into many small canals, and it turns out none of them leads to the Gulf—he becomes very disillusioned, but refuses to give up, because even though the original plan was one he made on a whim, once he has started something, he can't give up.

Summary and Analysis of Chapters 6-9

Soon after leaving Jan, McCandless sets up camp in the Anza-Borrego Desert State Park. One day while hiking back from a provisions trip he gets a ride from an eighty-year old man named Ronald Franz. Franz thinks that McCandless seems like a good person, and, thinking he's an uneducated bum, wants to encourage him to get his life together, but McCandless tells Franz that he already has a college education, and lives this way by choice.

Over the next few weeks McCandless and Franz spend a lot of time together, and Chris tells Franz that he is biding his time until spring, when he will go to Alaska. Soon after Chris gets a ride from Franz into San Diego, where he hopes to earn some money for his Alaska trip, but he has trouble finding work. He hops trains north to Seattle still looking for work, but isn't able to, so returns to California where he has Franz pick him up. McCandless has heard from Wayne Westerberg that he can work for him in Carthage, so Franz offers to drive him as close to it as he can without missing an appointment he has.

They spend a few days driving to Colorado together, and Franz finds himself very sad and lonely once McCandless leaves him, having become very attached to him. He gets a long letter from McCandless soon after, encouraging him to get out on the road and live like he does, and Franz takes this advice. Franz waits for McCandless's return, but one day when he picks up two hitchhikers and tells them about his friend "Alex," they tell him that they just read an article in *Outside* magazine about it, and he's dead. In response, Franz renounces God, and buys his first bottle of whiskey in a long time.

McCandless turns up in Carthage looking for work, and once again is happy to do all of the least desirable jobs at the grain elevator. He becomes close to Gail Borah, Westerberg's girlfriend, and tells her things he hasn't shared with anyone in awhile. Westerberg doesn't ask about McCandless's family, but he has a feeling that, knowing McCandless, he just got stuck on something that happened with his father and couldn't let it go.

In fact, both Walt and Chris are stubborn and high-strung, which leads to a great clash between them. Walt tries to control Chris, who is fiercely independent, and so he resents it deeply. Shortly before disappearing, Chris tells his sister, Carine, that he intends to soon cut off all relations with his parents, for good, disgusted by their attempts to control him and what he sees as their immoral lifestyle.

As McCandless prepares to leave Carthage for Alaska, he tells Westerberg that he will return there in the fall to help on the grain elevator again, and Westerberg gets the sense that his Alaska trip will be his last big adventure before he settles down, at least comparatively. Before leaving, McCandless has dinner with Westerberg's mother, Mary, with whom he really hits it off, and goes out one last time with

Westerberg's crew. He then heads off to Alaska.

Krakauer explains that he received a lot of negative mail after the original article about McCandless ran in *Outside* magazine, largely from Alaskans who thought McCandless didn't respect the wilderness, and acted stupidly and stubbornly. There were a few others notorious in Alaska for similar things, including Gene Rosellini, a brilliant man who had decided to see if man could still live as in pre-technology days, and survived without any tools but those he could make himself for over a decade, until he killed himself.

Another young man, John Waterman, is often compared to McCandless. He was a very talented young climber with a troubled relationship with his father, a tragic personal life, and a very eccentric personality. He became more and more unhinged, and eventually embarked on a borderline suicidal climb of Denali, during which he disappeared, and is presumed dead. Carl McCunn is also often compared to McCandless. He was an amateur photographer from Texas who moved to Alaska in the 1970s, and in 1981 arranged to be flown into the wilderness for five months, where he planned to mostly shoot pictures of wildlife. He forgot, however, to arrange to be picked up, and so ended up killing himself as he slowly and painfully starved and froze to death.

Everett Ruess was another figure who can be compared to Christopher McCandless. He was born in 1914 in California, and went on his first extended solo trip hitchhiking and trekking at the age of sixteen. With a few short exceptions, Ruess would spend the rest of his life on the move, living out of a backpack with very little money, often sleeping outside and making due with little food. He wrote many letters while doing this, which show his intense passion for nature and natural beauty.

Like McCandless, Ruess was very romantic, heedless of his personal safety, and undeterred by physical discomfort. He also changed his name, repeatedly, while journeying, finally etching "NEMO" into the sandstone at Davis Gulch twice, before disappearing forever at the age of twenty. His burros and their gear were found, but nothing else, and it is widely believed that he fell to his death while climbing on some canyon wall. Some, however, believe he just chose to disappear, and lived the rest of his life under a pseudonym. Ken Sleight, an expert on him, believes he drowned trying to swim across the San Juan River.

Analysis

In this section, many of the important themes of the book become apparent. In Ronald Franz we see another example, probably the strongest one, of someone who quickly becomes very attached to McCandless. With Franz it is so extreme that he asks to adopt McCandless, and changes his lifestyle completely, following Chris's advice. Yet this also, somewhat painfully, puts McCandless's selfishness in stark relief—although he accepts a fair amount of help from Franz, he leaves him before too much can be expected from him, and McCandless's death causes the old man to lose his strong faith in God, and to take up drinking again. This illuminates the actual costs of McCandless's risky behavior, not just to himself but to those who care for him.

We also start to see some of the reasons for McCandless's estrangement from his family. Although in some ways it seems like his choice to cut himself off from his family is an important part of his plan to have true freedom, it becomes clear in this section that in some ways it is intended specifically to punish them. He tells Carine soon before he disappears that he intends to cut his parents out of his life completely, because he resents their values, and their attempts to impose those values on him.

It is also interesting to see in this section how McCandless's expectations for his parents are so much higher than for other people in his life. He holds himself to these same standards, always living by the philosophies he espouses, and the standards he holds others to, but he is forgiving of many sins from his friends, including alcoholism and mistreatment of women. Yet even the offer to buy him a car as a graduation gift, coming from his parents, is enough to make him completely disgusted with them, even though, with Carine for example, he does not hold her materialism against her.

In the previous section, McCandless attempts a few times to rejoin society, but finds he cannot stomach it for long. Here we see, however, that he does seem to be planning to settle down after his Alaska trip—his last great adventure. Although it is tragically impossible to know whether he would've actually settled down, that he was planning on it at all shows that he did not see his lifestyle as a permanent one, and it also refutes on some level the idea that his Alaska trip was intentionally suicidal.

This section is also the first time Krakauer describes the other famous and infamous characters to whom McCandless is now often compared. Krakauer makes his own beliefs clear—that though McCandless shares some characteristics and behaviors with these men, the only one who is truly like him is Everett Ruess. Carl McCunn was more naïve, John Waterman was actually mentally insane, but Everett Ruess was, like McCandless, simply deeply in love with the land, very romantic, and passionate about living by his principles. These comparisons show that removing oneself from society and living riskily can be a symptom of insanity or stupidity, but it is not inherently so.

This in turn emphasizes the need to look deeply into something before passing judgment. Those who compare McCandless to John Waterman, for example, are doing so based on a few parallels, but a detailed study of either character very quickly shows that their motivations and behaviors were very different indeed. This highlights the purpose of *Into the Wild* itself, which is not just to tell an adventure story, but to study McCandless in the closest possible detail, so that is anyone is to pass judgment, it is at least with all the necessary information.

Summary and Analysis of Chapters 10-11

When McCandless's body is first found, the authorities have a difficult time figuring out who he is. An article runs about the unidentified body being found in the *Anchorage Daily News*, and Jim Gallien sees it, and is fairly sure it is "Alex," so he calls the state troopers. They show him the developed pictures from the camera, which Gallien immediately recognizes as McCandless, and so because he had told Gallien he was from South Dakota, the troopers start looking there for his next of kin.

The troopers find nothing in South Dakota, but Wayne Westerberg is alerted to a radio broadcast about the hiker by a friend, and agrees that it sounds like McCandless, so he too contacts the Alaska state troopers. On one of his employment forms, McCandless had put his real name and social security number, and from that the troopers find that he was from Virginia.

The McCandlesses have by then moved out of state, but Chris's half-brother Sam still lives in state, and receives a call from a local homicide detective about the unidentified hiker. He thinks it is likely that the hiker is his half-brother, and when he goes to the station to see a picture, he has no doubt. He then has to drive to Maryland to tell Walt and Billie that Chris is dead.

Seven weeks after Chris's body is found, Krakauer goes to Walt and Billie's Maryland home to talk to them. Walt is very authoritative, brilliant, and intense, and according to the family has a mercurial temper, which has mellowed greatly since Chris's disappearance. Walt started dating Billie, a secretary at his company, soon after his separation from his first wife, Marcia. They moved in together, and Billie got pregnant with Chris, who was born slightly underweight but healthy. From the beginning Chris was unusually gifted, and incredibly willful. He was never antisocial, but he was always content to be alone, without toys or anything but himself.

When Walt quits working at NASA to start his own company, money becomes a lot tighter and Walt and Billie have to work incredibly long hours, and the stress sometimes comes out in fights between Walt and Billie. They also have many happy moments, however, especially when travelling—McCandless's wanderlust begins early. Chris easily got A's in school, with the exception of an F in Physics when he refuses to do the lab reports according to the teacher's specifications because he thinks it is pointless. Chris also shows his musical talent from a young age. Chris and his younger sister, Carine, are very close, best friends all through childhood.

Throughout his life, Chris shows natural talent in many things, but always a strong resistance to being coached. He would get very skilled at different sports, but always refuses to follow instructions that could take him that last bit further to greatness. He doesn't like nuance or strategy, but only wants to tackle problems head on with brute strength and energy, which often leads to frustration. Running, which is more about will and determination than finesse or cunning, is a perfect match for him.

Even in high school McCandless is caught up in serious questions, becoming obsessed with fighting racial oppression in South Africa, and spending weekends in the seedier neighborhoods of Washington, D.C., talking to prostitutes and homeless people, buying them food and giving them earnest advice on how they can improve their lives. One time he even brings a homeless person home with him and secretly sets him up in the trailer his parents have beside their house.

Chris tells his parents he doesn't want to go to college, but they are insistent and end up convincing him. He also always is embarrassed by their wealth, even though both his parents have known poverty, have worked hard to gain what they have, and aren't flashy about it. But Chris thinks wealth is inherently evil, even though he is a natural salesman and capitalist from early on.

Analysis

This section makes very clear the consequences on everyone else for McCandless's stubborn carelessness about his own safety. As friend after friend hears about the unidentified hiker found dead in the Alaskan wilderness and becomes sure that it is McCandless, his carelessness stops seeming just stupid or foolhardy, but it starts to seem actually cruel, and this is especially emphasized when Krakauer visits McCandless's parents at their home, and sees firsthand the pain that Chris's disappearance and death has caused them.

In these chapters, Chris's childhood is also illuminated, and Krakauer traces back those characteristics that would lead to him deserting his family and all his possessions to wander into the wilderness. The strongest of these is his stubbornness, which prevents him from taking his talent to the next level in almost anything, because he is so against following directions and taking advice, or following authority. He is able to excel at running because he certainly has determination and natural athleticism, but at sports that require technique and finesse, he falls just short of greatness. This certainly seems to foreshadow what will happen to him in Alaska—his determination helps him survive for months under incredibly difficult conditions, but holes in his knowledge and his refusal to accept help eventually lead to his death.

Seeing this stubbornness in its youthful form illuminates certain qualities of it that would otherwise be unclear. What will become his passion and independence in his early twenties come off as simple aversion to authority in his younger years. Although he easily gets A's throughout most of his education, he fails a physics class, simply because he refuses to follow the teacher's specific guidelines for lab reports. The teacher institutes this policy because of the large number of reports he must grade, but to Chris—not quite capable of seeing it from someone else's perspective—it is just an arbitrary rule that someone wants to impose on him.

This also highlights the issue of perspective. Authority and rules feel utterly oppressive to McCandless, and he is so insistent on his own independence that he finds those who care about him giving him advice or showing concern over his safety to be an affront. Yet were he capable of seeing it from their perspective, he would understand that they just fear for what might happen to him, and for the great loss they would face as a result. And rules, though limiting in freedom, are what keep society running, and help all, not just the strongest, survive.

It becomes clear that this distaste for authority largely comes from the fact that he is—and always was—very independent and strong willed, and because his father is the same way, and tries to exert control over him, the two clash often and passionately. It seems that this is one of the primary reasons that McCandless's moral standards for his parents are so much higher than for others. He feels that, if his father is going to be in a position of authority over him, he had better be, essentially, perfect.

McCandless's passion for helping others and his distaste for materialistic society also show themselves very early. It is especially noteworthy that he doesn't just try to help people from a safe distance, but he actually drives into dangerous neighborhoods to talk to the homeless people, the prostitutes and drug addicts, to try to find ways to help them. For someone raised in the suburbs, this is especially unusual, and it shows how even at a very young age, he was not afraid of very much, and he was willing to venture far outside of his comfort zone—certainly a unique character.

Summary and Analysis of Chapters 12-13

After graduation, Chris's parents throw him a party, and he gives his dad an expensive telescope and a moving speech of thanks. He then leaves for his first road trip, which takes him across the country, and lasts until two days before the fall semester starts at Emory. He returns back thirty pounds lighter, and very scruffy looking. Near the end of his trip, he had gotten lost in the Mojave Desert, and almost died of dehydration. When Walt tries to encourage Chris to exercise more caution in the future, Chris bristles at this, and becomes even more unforthcoming about his plans.

As the school year goes on, Chris seems thrilled to be at Emory, returning to his clean cut look, taking pride in his grades, and even talking excitedly about plans to go to law school. That summer, Chris works for his parents' firm, and develops a flawless computer program, but refuses to tell his father how it works. Some of his darker qualities seem to intensify while he's at college, and when his friends start joining fraternities and sororities, he pulls into himself and becomes more self-absorbed and impatient with social interaction.

He spends the summer after his sophomore year delivering pizzas for Dominos, keeping careful track of his earnings, and becoming more withdrawn from and hostile towards his parents, for no reason that they can deduce. It turns out that the smoldering anger is fueled by a discovery Chris had made on his road trip after graduation, when he had gone to the neighborhood where he had spent his earliest years. Here, he gets enough information to piece together that his father had continued his relationship with his first wife in secret long after falling in love with Billie and fathering Chris, even fathering another son with her.

Chris doesn't tell anyone about this discovery, but instead broods about it, letting the negative feelings build up more and more over time. Chris's very strict moral code means that he is very unforgiving of his parents' faults and failings, even though he often forgives his artistic heroes or close friends of equally or more profoundly immoral behaviors. As Chris's resentment towards his parents grows, so too does it towards the rest of the world, as he starts to, for example, complain constantly about all the rich kids at Emory.

Interestingly, although Chris's academic interests and passions grow more and more towards issues like poverty, racism, and world hunger, he declares himself an ardent fan of Ronald Reagan, and co-founds a College Republican Club at Emory. He works on Emory's newspaper, and publishes many editorials, all impassioned, and voicing opinions that go all over the map. Chris has fewer and fewer friends as time passes, and those whom he keeps notice that with every month he becomes more intense.

The summer after his junior year, Chris goes off in his car again, and this time only sends his parents two postcards the whole time, one saying he is off to Guatemala, the next saying he is about to leave Fairbanks, and will be back in a few weeks. He returns in time for fall classes, and he spends his senior year living off campus in a spartanly furnished apartment, with no phone, and seeing almost no one outside of classes.

At graduation, Chris seems happy, and implies that he'll be traveling for the summer again, but leads his parents to think he'll visit them in Annandale before he leaves. He doesn't, and it is the last time they ever see him. As months and then years pass, the family's worry is extreme, and Billie never leaves the house without leaving a note for Chris on the door. In July of 1992, Billie wakes up in the middle of the night, completely convinced she has heard Chris calling for her to help him.

Carine also clashes fiercely with Walt and Billie as an adolescent, but she makes her peace with them soon after Chris's disappearance, and they are able to maintain a very good relationship. Sam McCandless calls her husband, Chris Fish, at work to tell him that Chris's body has been found, and Fish comes home to tell Carine that her brother is dead. Carine and Fish go to her parents' house, then fly to Fairbanks to bring home Chris's remains.

Analysis

Many of the people who reacted strongly to the story of McCandless's death were angered by what they perceived as his hubris, walking into the wilderness with few survival tools and almost no food, and no safety net. In this section, we see evidence that there is indeed some truth to this idea. It may have only been his youth, but although McCandless acknowledged the danger of his plan, he did not seem to truly believe that he wouldn't survive. On McCandless's first independent road trip, he gets lost in the Mojave desert and almost dies from dehydration. Yet, instead of learning a lesson from this, he instead is angered when his parents ask him to be more careful, offended at the idea that he can't take care of himself. This foreshadows McCandless's later insistence on going forward with his Alaska trip, against much advice, and without help, though it is often offered.

It is also on this trip that he makes the discovery that seems to push him over the edge from passionate and a little eccentric to extreme. While in California, he learns that his father had a double life for many years, and his parents lied to him about it growing up. Interestingly, when he returns from this trip, he seems more interested in school and a normal future than he did before, but once he moves back in with his parents for the summer with this knowledge of their secrets, his anger seethes, and he starts to resent his parents more and more.

This resentment also spreads to the society that his parents are part of. Although they both grew up poor and made their own money, he has always looked down on them for their materialism, and when he learns of their dishonesty, he starts to feel strong antipathy towards anyone with a lot of money. His growing intensity about the things he is passionate about isolates him from almost everyone he knew at Emory, and he resents them for their participation in the Greek life, which he finds distasteful.

This results in McCandless being almost completely isolated at Emory by his senior year. As we have seen, from his childhood on he has been content to be alone, with only his imagination to keep him busy, but this lack of interaction in this case allows his eccentricities to intensify even more, as he has little contact with those who might help him to mellow out, or at least distract him with the intricacies of social interaction. Without these, he has little to do but study and fixate on what he believes is the right way to live. This emphasizes once again the importance of perspective—without having the benefit of anyone else's perspective, McCandless has no way of sensing that all of his ideas and philosophies may not be right.

Thus, although there is much to admire in McCandless's passion, in his always practicing what he preaches, and doing his best to always live by his morals and by the standards that he sets for himself and or society at large, it becomes clear in this section that a lot of this passion has for its source bitterness, anger and resentment, and thus it is not purely admirable. There are, of course, much worse things to do with resentment, and McCandless does maintain his desire to help others, especially the hungry and poor, but the fact that this anger is at the root of his passion seems to at least partially explain why he has so much trouble with intimacy later, and why he does not temper the danger of his actions for the sake of those who love him. This anger thus seems to be a tragic flaw, which will lead to his downfall.

Summary and Analysis of Chapters 14-15

Krakauer, like McCandless, was a willful, self-absorbed, passionate, and moody child who had problems with male authority figures. He becomes obsessed with climbing in his late teens, and spends all of his time fantasizing about, planning and undertaking dangerous climbs. At twenty-three, he plans on an especially dangerous climb in Alaska, the Devils Thumb, and determines that he will go it alone. He is dimly aware that he might be getting in over his head, but that is part of the point, and only encourages his zeal.

He quits his carpentry job in Colorado, and drives off to Alaska. To get to the Thumb required either a jet or a boat, so he abandons his car and gets passage on a workboat. Krakauer arrives in Petersburg, the nearest town, and meets a woman named Kai, who invites him home for dinner and gives him a place to sleep. He starts on his journey to the peak the next day, totally alone. The first two days go well, and everything feels more melodramatic and extreme because of his solitude.

On the third day, just as he approaches the most dangerous and intimidating part yet, a snow storm breaks, and he loses all visibility. He twice almost falls into crevasses, and it takes him the entire day to make it through the dangerous icefall. Soon after, he reaches the place where a pilot is supposed to drop his food to him, but the unending snow means the conditions are too poor, so he just has to keep waiting as his supplies dwindle.

The plane finally comes, and though he is still mentally unprepared after the stress of waiting, the perfect weather the next day leads Krakauer to start the actual climb. He gets into a rhythm and makes significant progress, but all of a sudden he gets to a point where the ice that is supporting him has severely thinned out, and is impassable. He has no choice but to go back down.

The weather turns bad, and Krakauer is confined to the tent for three days. He quickly runs out of things to do, and so he smokes some marijuana he'd been planning to save to use as a kind of victory cigar. He throws the match into a bag of trash, which lights, and before he can put the fire out the inner wall of his tent is damaged, and the temperature inside is now thirty degrees colder. Even more than that, though, he is bothered by the fact that it is his father's tent, which had been loaned to him reluctantly.

Krakauer's relationship with his father, a fiercely competitive man who expects Jon to become a doctor, is very strained. Krakauer believes that only perfection will please his father, and he does his best to live up to these expectations, but when family secrets are revealed and he realizes his father himself is not perfect, his anger and resentment become extreme, and it is only decades later that he can accept his father as human. Lewis eventually develops post-polio syndrome, an extremely painful condition, and in an attempt to halt his decline, starts self-medicating. His misuse of the drugs ends up addling his mind, to the point where he has to be institutionalized, and no remnants of sanity are left.

When the weather clears, Krakauer decides to try to climb the Thumb again. This time he only makes it a hundred feet up before the weather forces him to stop, and his decent is terrifying and almost fatal. When he finally makes it back to his camp, he realizes that he is not going to be able to succeed, and he has to give up on climbing the north face of the Thumb. There is still an easier route, which he originally thought was beneath him, but which he now realizes is the only path he'll be able to succeed on, and so he tries that way.

When he wakes up the next morning, it is clear that the weather is not going to hold for very long, so he climbs as fast as he can with almost no gear, intending to go up and back before the storm hits. He reaches the summit after a quick and dangerous climb, takes a few pictures, and heads back down. He makes it back, and not too much later is back in Colorado, working the same construction job that he'd been at before he left.

Analysis

It is only in these sections that Krakauer truly becomes a character in *Into the Wild*, more than just narrator, investigator and interviewer. In his story of climbing the Devils Thumb, he illuminates a lot of parallels between himself and McCandless, and we see how he probably can understand McCandless's motivations deeply, without having ever met him, because of their similarities in life circumstances and personalities. This does raise the question, however, of if he can really tell this story impartially, or might he be imposing his own story onto McCandless's, which, with his death, can never be completely known.

This draws attention to the problem of biography generally, that someone has to write it, and by choosing what to put in and what to leave out, how to frame the story, and how to tell it, the biographer has significant control over how the public will perceive the subject of the biography. In this case especially, where much is not known and the key figure is deceased, there is more room for the biographer to assert his own perspective. Yet Krakauer does it explicitly—he admits that he may be impartial, that he feels a connection to McCandless, and he makes explicit where he is making assumptions or drawing conclusions that cannot be proven.

This switch to Krakauer's story, taking Krakauer from journalist, author and narrator to subject and temporary protagonist, highlights again the issue of point-of-view and perspective. Not only does this section emphasize Krakauer's impartiality and personal perspective, but it also highlights the fact that, unlike Krakauer, McCandless will never be able to tell his own story. We must rely on Krakauer's perspective of everything that happened to McCandless because we will never have McCandless's, and this again emphasizes the tragedy of his death.

The inclusion of Krakauer's own story in *Into the Wild* does seem to complicate McCandless's story, and allows us to see, if not into McCandless's mind, at least into the mind of someone who had similar passions, demons, and ambitions. Krakauer's loneliness in his time on Devils Thumb seems significant, as McCandless chose to go into the Alaskan wilderness alone, and while he generally seemed to bask in his independence and solitude, Krakauer's admission that as much as he thought he could do without people, he was really lonely, makes it seem likely that McCandless probably had moments of deep loneliness as well.

Krakauer's story also makes it clear that McCandless was almost surely not suicidal. Although he admits, in his last postcard to Westerberg, that he is aware that he might never make it out of the wilderness alive, he believes in his ability to survive, and he is too young to truly be able to imagine death, especially because he has managed to survive all of his other dangerous adventures. Krakauer does not give up on his ascent even after multiple near-death encounters, for he has put so much stake on succeeding that to give up is unimaginable, and it seems likely that for a similar reason, no matter the advice he got, McCandless cannot imagine changing or giving up on his Alaska plan.

Krakauer does eventually give up on his first ascent plan, going up an easier way instead, and this amounts to a discovery that is difficult for both he and McCandless to accept—there are some things that, no matter your will or determination, are impossible. The same is not true of McCandless's adventure—he did survive for many, many weeks with minimal supplies in dangerous conditions, and he very conceivably could have made it out alive. But his way of thinking, that he can do anything as long as he truly has the determination to do it, and is willing to suffer while doing it, is not, in the end, correct.

Summary and Analysis of Chapter 16

On April 15, 1992, McCandless leaves Carthage and begins his hitchhiking journey to Alaska. After a few days he gets to the start of the Alaska Highway in Canada, where he takes a picture in front of the sign at mile zero—1,523 miles from Fairbanks. Although hitchhiking on the Alaska Highway is known to be difficult, McCandless manages to get a ride quickly. On April 21 he arrives at Laird River Hotsprings, a popular stop on the Alaska Highway, but after trying out the thermal pools, McCandless finds he can't get another ride, and days go by.

McCandless meets Gaylord Stuckey, a sixty-three year old man who is driving an RV to a dealership in Fairbanks, in the thermal pools one morning. Although Stuckey's job strictly forbids picking up hitchhikers, he takes a liking to McCandless, and offers to drive him at least part of the way. After a day and a half he has really come to enjoy his company, and so tells him he'll drive him the whole way to Fairbanks.

Over the long ride, McCandless opens up to Stuckey, and talks mostly about Carine, but also how his father is a brilliant scientist, but had been a bigamist at one point, which McCandless couldn't stomach. He tells Stuckey about his Alaska plan, and when they get to Fairbanks he buys a bag of rice at the grocery store, and tells Stuckey he wants to go to the University to study what kind of plants he'll be able to eat. Stuckey tells McCandless that he's too early, there's still two or three feet of snow on the ground, but McCandless is too stubborn to listen.

In the campus book store, McCandless finds an exhaustive guide to edible plants of the region, and buys two postcards on which he sends his last messages to Jan Burres and Wayne Westerberg. He finds a used gun and some shells to buy, and then after about two days in Fairbanks, packs up his bag and heads west, and camps for the night. The next morning, the first car he sees picks him up, and Jim Gallien takes him to the edge of the wilderness. When Gallien drops McCandless off, there is about a foot and a half of snow on the ground, and the high temperature is in the low thirties.

The only food McCandless has with him is a ten pound bag of rice and Jim Gallien's lunch, but he believes this will be enough because of his experience surviving in Mexico for over a month with only a five pound bag of rice, and fish he was able to catch himself with a cheap rod. He carries about nine or ten books with him, but not a journal, so when he writes he just uses some blank pages in the back of his books.

After two days, McCandless reaches the Teklanika River. There is still ice, but nowhere does it span the whole river, so he is forced to wade across. Because of the conditions, this is easy, and there is nothing to hint to him that in a few months, after further thawing, it will be uncrossable. A few days later he stumbles across the old bus, which is stocked with some essentials, so he decides to stay there for a little while and take advantage of its comforts. He is ecstatic to be alone in the wild.

McCandless is quickly faced with reality, however. He has trouble killing game, and quickly becomes weak and very hungry. By mid-May, however, his luck turns, as the weather gets better, the snow melts, and he can start foraging for rose hips and lingonberries. He also becomes more successful at hunting, and regularly shoots squirrels, grouse, duck, goose, and porcupine. His original intention is to stay moving, so on May 5 he leaves the bus and starts traveling.

It quickly becomes clear that this will not be easy, as McCandless has to spend much of each day hunting, and the ground is boggy and marshy. After two weeks, he has only traveled fifteen miles, so he turns around and within a week is back at the bus, deciding to use it as a base camp for the rest of the summer. Although this is not actually that far from civilization, it is sufficiently isolated that for the four months he spends there, he never comes across another human.

McCandless has a few weeks of great hunting, and then manages to kill a moose. He believes it is morally necessary to use every part of the moose and not waste any of it, so he spends the next few days desperately trying to preserve all of the hundreds of pounds of meat. Alaskan hunters know that air drying is the best way to preserve meat there, but McCandless relies on advice he received from hunters in South Dakota, who recommended smoking the meat. He ends up having to leave almost all of it to the wolves, and he deeply regrets having wasted the moose's life.

He comes to accept the loss, and based on a list he makes of things to do before he departed, it seems clear that he is preparing to return to civilization, and perhaps even join society. A photo he takes of himself at around this time, after shaving for the first time in the wilderness, shows him looking healthy, but already alarmingly gaunt. He packs up all of his gear and starts his hike back to the road that brought him here, but he comes across a three-acre lake covering the trail, where before there was only ice and small ponds. He manages to climb around this, but when he reaches the Teklanika River, he finds what was easily crossed in April is now a rushing torrent which would surely drown him, so he turns back, hoping if he waits it out it will again become crossable.

Analysis

Throughout McCandless's years on the road, when people meet him, they usually assume at first that he is uneducated and is an itinerant worker by necessity, not by choice. One of the ways in which McCandless is different from someone who lives that way by necessity is the ambition he exhibits, even in a rootless, anti-materialist life. This is evidenced when, although he has no deadline, no need to get to Alaska by a certain time, he becomes extremely impatient when delayed on the Alaska Highway, as though he has an important deadline to meet.

As we also saw when he tried to canoe to the Gulf of California, even when trying to accomplish something decided on a whim, he is incredibly persistent, and will not easily give up. Although he may not have ambitions to climb the ladder of capitalist American society, he certainly is ambitious. This parallels with Krakauer's story in the previous section, for he realized that his own mountain climbing ambition, though not at all what his father wanted for him, was still ambition, and was as extreme as his father's ambition, just in a different incarnation. This once again highlights the importance of perspective, for what is a valuable and ambitious goal for one person seems foolhardy and useless to another.

McCandless getting picked up by Gaylord Stuckey for the whole ride to Fairbanks is another example of someone going the extra mile for him. Stuckey agrees to drive him even though, with his work, it is expressly forbidden, and he could lose his job if he is caught. Yet, like so many others, he is charmed by McCandless, and so he agrees to give him a ride. This on the one hand emphasizes that there was something deeply special about McCandless, yet it also emphasizes that although McCandless was so insistent on independence, he very often relied on others, on the kindness of strangers, and almost everyone he came across did far more than the bare minimum to help him—like Jim Gallien, who gave him not only a ride, but also his lunch and his boots.

As Gallien drives McCandless to his drop off point, McCandless gets very excited, and his journal entries and photographs show that when he gets to the bus which will become his final home, he is ecstatic to be alone in the wilderness. The day to day effort of trying to find food and stay alive quickly sets in, however, and the reality of living this extreme way takes away from the romance of it. His notebook is almost exclusively about what he ate every day, for the effort to stay alive is so all consuming that there is little time for contemplating the serenity, for philosophizing on the wilderness. The difference between this, and for example, the writing of Jack London which he loves so much, shows that there is much more room for romance in literature than in reality. There is also a certain irony in this difference, especially as Jack London himself barely spent any time in the wild.

McCandless does seem to undergo some changes, though, beyond the physical losing weight. He is devastated when he kills a moose and then has to essentially waste all of it because he can't preserve it successfully, yet he fairly quickly realizes that he has to let this disappointment go, which is a new and more mature reaction from the intensely passionate man. Similarly, his original plan is to spend the time in the wilderness on the move, perhaps hiking almost five hundred miles, but when after a week or two of trying to move every day, he realizes this is much more difficult and slow going than he expected, he heads back to the bus, and doesn't seem nearly as upset with having to give up or change his plans as he would've been in the past, for example, with his Mexico trip. Although these are fairly small examples, they hint at McCandless becoming a more dynamic character, capable of learning, growing and changing.

Summary and Analysis of Chapters 17-18 and Epilogue

A year after McCandless wanted to cross the river, Krakauer stands on the other side, also wanting to cross, with three companions. Krakauer has a map that shows that there is a gauging station only half a mile downstream, which has a wire crossing the river, and a basket that one can ride across in. When they get to the station, they see that the basket is on the far side of the river, and it had been there when McCandless wanted to cross—had he known about it, he easily could have crossed to safety. McCandless, however, wanted to be on uncharted territory, and so didn't carry a good map with him.

Because the basket is on the other side, Krakauer uses his rock climbing hardware to pull himself across the wire. He then gets into the basket and heads back to the other side to ferry his companions across. Before crossing the river, the trail was well-marked and fairly easy, but on the other side it is overgrown and indistinct, since so few people cross the river in the spring. It is never exceedingly difficult, but many parts of the trek are unpleasant, and it has a kind of malevolent feel to it.

At nine pm they come upon the bus, which is an appealing spot, open and filled with light. The bus is surrounded by lots of tiny bones from the small game that McCandless ate, as well as the skeleton of the moose that he so regretted killing. Gordon Samel and Ken Thompson had insisted the McCandless misidentified the moose, and that it was really a caribou, which led many readers of Krakauer's *Outside* article to insist that McCandless was ill-prepared and ignorant. On close study of the remains, however, it becomes clear that it is, indeed, a moose.

Inside the bus, they find some of McCandless's leftover possessions, as well as a bag of feathers he had stored away, probably to insulate his clothes or make a pillow. There is lots of graffiti in the bus from all those who have stayed in it, but McCandless's etchings are by far the longest. Leaving the bus, Krakauer and his companions make camp, and discuss why so many people seem to hate McCandless so intensely for having died there. Many find his lack of what they consider necessary provisions to be a sign of his profound arrogance.

Some have even compared him to Sir John Franklin, a nineteenth century British naval officer. On the first trip he leads through the wilderness of northwestern Canada, eleven men end up dead from starvation, sickness, and murder, and all are only days from starving when they are rescued. Because he survives, he is promoted, but his lack of survival skills and his unwillingness to acquire any meant that when he chooses to go on another Arctic expedition, this time leading 128 men, not one of them is ever heard from again.

Although McCandless did lack some knowledge and skills that could have helped him, it oversimplifies matters to blame his arrogance and ignorance for his death, for he does manage to survive for sixteen weeks with only ten pounds of rice and very few tools. He also is well aware how slim a margin of error he has given himself. Krakauer and his companions stay up late into the night discussing McCandless, what made him tick, and so on. They finally go to bed, not sure whether they have come any closer to the truth.

McCandless returns to the bus on July 8, and his diary says nothing about how his state of mind is. He continues to be successful hunting, however the small game he catches does not have much in it, and he runs up a caloric deficit, continuing to lose weight. He reads *Doctor Zhivago*, and makes many notes in the margins, some of which hint that he is getting ready to rejoin the human community, and perhaps stop avoiding intimacy.

Before July 30, there is nothing in McCandless's diary to hint that he is in anything but good health, if a little undernourished, but on July 30 he writes that he is extremely weak and having trouble even standing up. There are several theories as to what caused the change. One food that McCandless has been taking advantage of is a kind of wild potato, but by mid-July they might have been becoming too tough to eat, and it's possible he started ingesting the seed pods of the plant instead. In addition, there is a kind of wild pea that looks very similar to the potato, but is poisonous. Krakauer believes that the former was the case, as McCandless had successfully eaten the potato for weeks without mistaking the pea for it, and there is a picture showing him with a bag of seeds—he even writes in his journal that his illness is the fault of the "pot. seed."

However, when Krakauer sends samples of the seeds to be tested, no traces of poisons are found. Krakauer later finds an article about a dangerous mold that can grow on such plants in wet climates, and believes that this, in fact, is what killed McCandless.The moldy seeds make the already weak McCandless incapable of climbing back to civilization or hunting, which leads to further weakness. There are three cabins, all stocked with some first aid gear and provisions, within six miles of McCandless's bus, but he doesn't know they exist. It turns out, however, that a vandal had destroyed all three cabins recently anyway, so the provisions inside them would have been ruined, even if McCandless knew of their existence and could have reached them.

Over the next days, McCandless manages to shoot small game here and there, and forage for some berries, but the poison in his system makes this food useless. His diary entries become fewer and farther between, and he finally rips a page out of one of his books containing a poem about death, and writes a goodbye message on the back—"I HAVE HAD A HAPPY LIFE AND THANK THE LORD. GOODBYE AND MAY GOD BLESS ALL!" He takes a last picture of himself in front of the bus, holding his farewell note, and then crawls into his sleeping bag and at some point in the next few days, dies.

Ten months after learning of Chris's death, Walt and Billie decide to go to see the place where he died. They plan to go overland as Chris did, but the river is still too high, and so with Krakauer they take a helicopter to the bus. Billie says the area reminds her of where she grew up on the Upper Peninsula, and thinks that Chris must have loved it. Walt grudgingly admits that it has a certain beauty. They put a small memorial plaque on the bus, and Billie leaves a first aid kit with a note to whoever finds it to call their parents as soon as possible.

Analysis

The final section of *Into the Wild* is especially tragic, in that it shows that McCandless, at least from what little evidence is available from his last weeks, had matured, and was ready to rejoin society. There is some evidence, in the notes he made in the books he read, for example, that he was rethinking his stance on forgiveness, and on intimacy, and would maybe have become capable of being close to other people again. Unfortunately, his ignorance about the condition of the Teklanika, his insistence on visiting "uncharted territory," by not brining a map, meant once he was ready, mentally and emotionally, to leave, he physically could not. In this we see another example of the motif of McCandless almost being saved, as had he only known about the basket crossing the Teklanika, he almost certainly would have survived.

Although many people looked down on McCandless for his Alaskan trip and the way he died, those who claim he was suicidal don't seem to have much to stand on, based on McCandless's writings and his attempt to leave the wilderness. And while he was ignorant of some things, he did manage to survive for four months, with almost no provisions, in the harsh Alaskan wilderness, so he clearly was at least capable, if not expert. In addition, the mistakes that were held against him as evidence of his arrogance and ignorance were in fact not mistakes that he made. Thus, although McCandless's death forever dooms him to be remembered as having failed to survive in the wilderness, he did come very close to having had a miraculously successful trip.

The comparison that some have made to Sir John Franklin is, thus, certainly not fair, although considering it does illuminate some things. The only true parallel is that both Franklin and McCandless did, after surviving a first close call, overestimate their own abilities, although Franklin's overestimation was much more extreme. In addition, Franklin's arrogance and ignorance were not dangerous and ultimately deadly only to himself—he was entrusted with the care of over a hundred men altogether, when he should have been fully aware that he could not even take care of himself in the wilderness. McCandless only had his own safety and health on his hands, and to risk this is certainly much less terrible than to risk the safety of others.

Yet, it should not be forgotten, as he seemed to have done himself, that there were many others whose well-being, if not direct safety, was resting on his care for himself. This may be part of why he avoided intimacy, for the more people relied on him, the more he would have to be responsible for himself. In taking the risks he did, while only his own safety was at stake, he was risking the happiness and peace of all of those who loved him. In isolating himself in the wilderness, he was attempting to cut all ties, but from the perspective of anyone who loved him, they were still worrying and thinking about him constantly, and thus not cut off in actuality at all. Thus, no matter how noble his goals and principles, it is impossible to see his actions without them being tinged with the selfishness inherent in them.

The closing section of *Into the Wild* ultimately makes clear that it is impossible to ever truly, fully understand another person. Krakauer spends three years researching McCandless's life and journeys, and he has many parallels in his own life to help him understand, but he still cannot, in the end, say with any certainty what ultimately led McCandless into the wild, and why he didn't survive the foray, but instead died, alone, at twenty-four. He cannot even say with absolutely certainty what killed McCandless. And although he attempts to find some answers by highlighting all the examples of times McCandless almost made a decision that could have saved him, in the end it is only conjecture, since this book is not fiction but fact, and can only have the ending which actually happened.

Suggested Essay Questions

1. **Is it possible for a biography to be truly impartial? Is *Into the Wild*?**

Biography can never be truly impartial, as, even if the author could include every moment of the subject's life, rather than choosing which are most important, his method of presentation and his diction, inherently affect how the reader will feel about the subject. There is still a scale of more or less impartial, however, and *Into the Wild* falls on the less-impartial side, as Krakauer himself admits. For example, because he sees a lot of similarities between Chris and himself, he makes certain assumptions about Chris's motivations and desires that he might not otherwise make. Yet because Krakauer makes this explicit, and doesn't try to fool the reader, the reader still has the freedom to make their own interpretation.

2. **Is McCandless truly compassionate, as he is often described?**

McCandless's compassion is the most enigmatic part of his story. It is clearly central to his personality for his whole life—he spends weekend nights in high school bringing burgers to homeless people—and yet he shows almost no compassion in dealing with his parents once he is in college. He willingly and intentionally leaves them in a state of utter unhappiness while he travels, and his disregard for his own safety threatens and ultimately destroys their wellbeing. This does not mean that he is not truly compassionate, but this compassion does have bounds.

3. **In Krakauer's depiction of McCandless, is he a flat or round character? Static or dynamic?**

In Krakauer's depiction, McCandless is certainly a round character. Although he is largely presented as good, his flaws are illuminated, and even his best qualities sometimes fail him. Krakauer also makes him a dynamic character, although the basis for this is largely conjecture. Krakauer believes that McCandless changed during his Alaska trip, that he may have mellowed and become ready to rejoin society and maybe even his family, although all of this is based on a few small lines Chris wrote, and passages he underlined in his reading.

4. **Explain how McCandless's quest for "ultimate freedom" is inherently selfish.**

McCandless's quest for ultimate freedom is not rooted in selfishness; it, in fact, comes out of largely noble desires. It is still inherently selfish, however, because it means acting for the individual over society, which is designed to protect everybody. Ultimate freedom means being accountable to no one but oneself, and thus, even if McCandless usually intended to act for the greater good, he has only his own limited perspective on what will truly lead to the greater good.

5. **How does Krakauer's authorial presence affect McCandless's story?**

Krakauer's own upbringing and experiences as a young man come up throughout *Into the Wild*. Because there are such strong similarities to McCandless, the biggest difference being that Krakauer survived his odysseys, and so can tell his tale, Krakauer uses his own past to provide insights into McCandless's actions and motivations. This also probably leads Krakauer to present McCandless in the most forgiving light that he can.

6. **What does *Into the Wild* posit as the core of the problems between McCandless and his father?**

Both Chris and Walt McCandless are strong-willed and independent, and Chris's resistance to all authority means that he resents the authority his father has over him, even as he tries to please him. Chris specifically detests arbitrary authority, and so once he has proof that his father isn't perfect, he then considers Walt's authority over him to be completely arbitrary, and he resists it absolutely. Because of Chris's intensity and tendency towards extremes, this becomes much more than just a typical adolescent rebellion.

7. **What specific appeal does the wilderness have for all the adventure seekers described in *Into the wild*?**

The adventure seekers in *Into the Wild* all seem to be searching for a life with a kind of brute simplicity, which they believe they can find in the wilderness. High-risk living leaves little time for the complicated problems of modern society, and this seems to be much of the appeal for these men. They also seem to believe that there is some core of truth hidden beneath all the layers of modern life, and this can only be found in the wild. Finally, surviving the challenges posed by this way of life provide a feeling of deep accomplishment for these often ambitious or competitive men.

8. **How is McCandless's difficulty forgiving a driving force in his journeys?**

McCandless, though largely driven by his principals and morals to live a rootless, anti-materialist existence, also seems at least partially driven forward by a desire to punish his parents. He resents their pressure for him to go to law school, their materialism, and what he sees as their attempts to control him, so he tells Carine that he is going to cut them out of his life completely because he cannot forgive them. In not contacting them at all while he is on the road, he turns his odyssey into a tool for punishment, at least on some level.

9. **How can McCandless's Datsun symbolize his interpersonal relationships?**

McCandless is completely committed to his Datsun from the time he buys it until he graduates from college, when he is deeply offended by his parents' offer to buy him a new car. He tells Carine that he would never trade in his Datsun, which he thinks is perfect. Once he has trouble with the car, though, he deserts it immediately and angrily. Chris loves the Datsun despite its surface flaws, just like he is able to love most of his friends regardless of their looks, money, or way of life, but when he perceives a deeper flaw, he is unforgiving, and cuts it out of his life completely, as he does with his parents.

10. **McCandless's story, despite its tragic end, has inspired many copycats since the original publication in *Into the Wild*. Why might this be?**

Krakauer presents McCandless's tale in a forgiving way, yet it is still a cautionary tale—although he believes Chris could have survived, and only died because of a small mistake, he shows just how devastating such behavior can be to McCandless, and to those who loved him. Yet McCandless's passion for living by his principals, for simplicity and purity, is attractive and to Krakauer, admirable, and the book does show that it may indeed be the wilderness that is the best place to find this. Thus, those who feel unsatisfied by modern life and society may see McCandless's flight from it as worthy of emulation.

McCandless's Copycats

Although *Into the Wild* was largely a cautionary tale, since its publication, many more young men have followed in McCandless's footsteps. With the book's great success, McCandless's bus has become a famous landmark, often a source of pilgrimage for those looking to challenge themselves, to connect with nature, and to reject society just as McCandless did.

Many locals of Healy, Alaska, fear that *Into the Wild* has romanticized the Alaskan bush in a way that is potentially dangerous, as these young men, who are often not very experienced outdoorsmen, try to mimic McCandless. Indeed, many of these people have ended up having to be rescued, and so town officials have considered removing the bus in an effort to dissuade these inexperienced pilgrims.

It is also interesting that, whereas McCandless was looking to truly go off the beaten path, and for that reason did not even carry a map, these men who copy him are following his path closely, and in so doing are not truly following his principles. As *Into the Wild* shows, McCandless clearly wasn't the only person to ever make great sacrifices to live in the wilderness, and many have done it before him, but it seems that the popularization of his tale has prompted some of those who might normally find less extreme ways of rejecting society to follow his far more dangerous path.

Author of ClassicNote and Sources

Alice Cullina, author of ClassicNote. Completed on August 20, 2009, copyright held by GradeSaver.

Updated and revised Damien Chazelle November 30, 2009. Copyright held by GradeSaver.

"About Jon Krakauer." Random House. 2009-08-09. <http://www.randomhouse.com/features/krakauer/author.html>.

Karlinsky, Neal. "'Into the Wild' Inspires Adventurers, but at What Cost?." ABC News: Nightline. 2007-10-15. 2009-08-08. <http://abcnews.go.com/Nightline/Story?id=3680748&page=1>.

Krakauer, Jon. "Death of an Innocent." Outside Magazine. 1993-01-01. 2009-08-11. <http://outside.away.com/outside/features/1993/1993_into_the_wild_1.html>.

Andriani, Lynn. "Krakauer's Tillman Book Due in September." Publishers Weekly. 2009-02-09. 2009-08-13. <http://www.publishersweekly.com/article/CA6636050.html>.

Bryson, George. "Theories Differ on the Cause of McCandless's Death." Anchorage Daily News. 2007-10-08. 2009-08-11. <http://www.adn.com/intothewild/story/219344.html>.

Quiz 1

1. **Who is the last person to see McCandless alive?**
   A. Gaylord Stuckey
   B. Wayne Westerberg
   C. Jim Gallien
   D. Gordon Samel

2. **What name does McCandless go by after leaving Atlanta?**
   A. Tolstoy
   B. Alex
   C. John
   D. Chris

3. **In what season does McCandless go into the wilderness?**
   A. Spring
   B. Summer
   C. Winter
   D. Fall

4. **What makes McCandless afraid of water?**
   A. A flash flood that almost drowns him in the Mojave Desert
   B. Falling into the ocean as a young child
   C. Almost drowning in his canoe in Mexico
   D. Drinking bad water that makes him sick in Alaska

5. **What does McCandless do in Bullhead City?**
   A. Stays in a monastery
   B. Canoes around
   C. Works on a farm
   D. Works at McDonalds

6. **Who does Krakauer think was most like McCandless?**
   A. John Waterman
   B. Everett Ruess
   C. Wayne Westerberg
   D. Carl McCunn

7. **Which of the following does not describe McCandless?**
   A. Stubborn
   B. Easy going
   C. Passionate
   D. Moral

8. **Which of the following does McCandless declare himself a fan of, which is surprising, considering his tastes and beliefs?**
   A. Tolstoy
   B. Jack London
   C. George H. W. Bush
   D. Ronald Reagan

9. **What is Krakauer's obsession in his early twenties?**
   A. Skiing
   B. Hunting
   C. Writing
   D. Mountain climbing

10. **What seems to lead to McCandless's total separation from his parents?**
    A. His discovery of his father's secret past
    B. Their divorce
    C. Their graduation gift of a car
    D. Their pushing him to go to law school

11. **In what is McCandless living at the end of his life?**
    A. A bus
    B. A treehouse
    C. A cave
    D. A tent

12. **What does McCandless do the summer after his sophomore year of college?**
    A. Drive to Mexico
    B. Deliver pizzas
    C. Volunteer at a homeless shelter
    D. Camp in Alaska

13. **What kind of car does Chris drive?**
    A. A Datsun
    B. A Toyota
    C. A Ford
    D. A Volkswagen

14. **Who of the following does not actually live an outdoorsy or adventurous life?**
    A. Everett Ruess
    B. Chris McCandless
    C. Jack London
    D. Jon Krakauer

15. **What does Ron Franz ask McCandless?**
    A. If he can come with him to Alaska
    B. If he can adopt him
    C. For him not to go through with the Alaska trip
    D. If he can meet his parents

16. **What do we know McCandless comes to regret deeply?**
    A. Not telling his parents where he is
    B. Killing the moose
    C. Not bringing more food with him into the wilderness
    D. Trying to shoot a bear with his small gun

17. **What prevents McCandless from leaving the wilderness on his first attempt?**
    A. He decides he can't handle readjusting to society
    B. The Teklanika River is uncrossable
    C. He gets too weak from food poisoning
    D. He can't find his way

18. **What does Wayne Westerberg say McCandless liked to drink?**
    A. White Russians
    B. Green tea
    C. White wine
    D. Beer

19. **If McCandless had had a good map with him in Alaska, what might he have seen?**
    A. An easy way to cross the Teklanika, only half a mile downstream
    B. A nearby hunting cabin where he could've found help
    C. An easy back way out of his camp to a nearby town
    D. An emergency radio station not far from the bus

20. **What does McCandless's Alaska journal largely contain?**
    A. Descriptions of the scenery
    B. Explanations for all of his choices
    C. Abstractions about nature and his own soul
    D. Lists of what he ate

21. **Why is McCandless's skill at making money surprising?**
    A. Because he is very bad with numbers
    B. Because he is an irresponsible spender
    C. Because he believes wealth is inherently evil
    D. Because he has trouble focusing on any one task

22. **Which extracurricular is McCandless involved in at Emory?**
    A. Cross country
    B. College Democrats Club
    C. The outdoors club
    D. Writing for the newspaper

23. **Who is the first in the family to find out about Chris's death?**
    A. Sam McCandless
    B. Walt McCandless
    C. Chris Fish
    D. Carine McCandless

24. **What was the only thing that would've pleased Krakauer's father?**
    A. Jon becoming a doctor
    B. Jon climbing the Devils Thumb
    C. Jon giving up climbing
    D. Jon becoming a policeman

25. What quality of Chris's does Carine not share?

A. Distaste for wealth

B. High-achiever

C. Having had a bad relationship with their parents

D. Intensity

Quiz 1 Answer Key

1. **(C)** Jim Gallien
2. **(B)** Alex
3. **(A)** Spring
4. **(C)** Almost drowning in his canoe in Mexico
5. **(D)** Works at McDonalds
6. **(B)** Everett Ruess
7. **(B)** Easy going
8. **(D)** Ronald Reagan
9. **(D)** Mountain climbing
10. **(A)** His discovery of his father's secret past
11. **(A)** A bus
12. **(B)** Deliver pizzas
13. **(A)** A Datsun
14. **(C)** Jack London
15. **(B)** If he can adopt him
16. **(B)** Killing the moose
17. **(B)** The Teklanika River is uncrossable
18. **(A)** White Russians
19. **(A)** An easy way to cross the Teklanika, only half a mile downstream
20. **(D)** Lists of what he ate
21. **(C)** Because he believes wealth is inherently evil
22. **(D)** Writing for the newspaper
23. **(A)** Sam McCandless
24. **(A)** Jon becoming a doctor
25. **(A)** Distaste for wealth

Quiz 2

1. **Where does McCandless go to college?**
   A. University of Alaska
   B. University of Virginia
   C. Yale
   D. Emory

2. **Who drives McCandless most of the way to Fairbanks on the Alaska Highway?**
   A. Gaylord Stuckey
   B. Wayne Westerberg
   C. Jim Gallien
   D. Ronald Franz

3. **What is the last book that McCandless reads?**
   A. Walden
   B. Jurassic Park
   C. Doctor Zhivago
   D. War and Peace

4. **Who of the following is at least partially responsible for the death of 140 people?**
   A. John Waterman
   B. Chris McCandless
   C. Sir John Franklin
   D. Leo Tolstoy

5. **About how much money does McCandless give to charity?**
   A. $5
   B. $500
   C. $25,000
   D. $100,000

6. **Why does McCandless end up staying at the bus, rather than keeping on the move?**
   A. After seeing a lot of grizzlies, he doesnâ'Žt want to sleep unprotected
   B. After killing the moose he has too much meat to carry with him, and he doesn't want to waste it
   C. The boggy ground makes for very slow going
   D. He has trouble orienting himself, and is worried about getting lost

7. Where does McCandless grow up?
A. Arizona
B. Virginia
C. California
D. South Dakota

8. Which of the following does McCandless not excel at?
A. The French horn
B. Running
C. Academics
D. Golf

9. What does Chris spend most of his time in Mexico doing?
A. Rock climbing
B. Surfing
C. Canoeing
D. Working on a farm

10. Where does McCandless die?
A. Mexico
B. Arizona
C. Virginia
D. Alaska

11. What is most likely responsible for McCandless's death?
A. Eating moose meat that had gone bad
B. Mistaking poisonous sweet pea roots for edible potato roots
C. Poisonous mold on potato seeds he ate
D. Poisonous potato seeds

12. Where does McCandless work in Las Vegas?
A. A soup kitchen
B. A casino
C. An Italian restaurant
D. Pizza Hut

13. **Who thinks that McCandless's body should be immediately evacuated?**
    A. Butch Killian
    B. Sam McCandless
    C. Carine McCandless
    D. Gordon Samel

14. **Which family member is closest to Chris?**
    A. Sam
    B. Walt
    C. Billie
    D. Carine

15. **What is McCandless known for when he works for Westerberg?**
    A. Always starting a new task before he had finished his last one
    B. Doing the jobs that no one else wanted
    C. Complaining a lot
    D. Being an especially fast worker

16. **Who launches a Presidential campaign?**
    A. John Waterman
    B. Everett Ruess
    C. Chris McCandless
    D. Wayne Westerberg

17. **How does Krakauer cross the Teklanika?**
    A. He crosses it when itâ'Žs frozen
    B. He uses an amphibious vehicle
    C. A cable running across the river
    D. He wades through it

18. **Which of these places does McCandless not visit during his two years on the road?**
    A. Bullhead City
    B. Las Vegas
    C. Winnetka
    D. Oh-My-God Hot Springs

19. **Who changes his or her lifestyle based on McCandless's advice?**
    A. Wayne Westerberg
    B. Carine McCandless
    C. Jim Gallien
    D. Ronald Franz

20. **How does McCandless ruin his first camera?**
    A. He leaves it outside during a storm
    B. It gets wet when he almost drowns in Mexico
    C. He drops it into the Grand Canyon
    D. He buries it unprotected

21. **Where is the Devils Thumb?**
    A. Russia
    B. Arizona
    C. Colorado
    D. Alaska

22. **What mistake did some Alaskans think McCandless made, that it turns out he did not?**
    A. Eating potato seeds even though they were moldy
    B. Trying to shoot a grizzly with a small gun
    C. Mistaking a caribou for a moose
    D. Trying to preserve meat by smoking it

23. **Who of the following is not presumed to have died in the wilderness?**
    A. John Waterman
    B. Everett Ruess
    C. John Muir
    D. Chris McCandless

24. **What club does McCandless co-found in college?**
    A. Distance Runners Club
    B. College Republican Club
    C. Transcendentalist Club
    D. Jack London Fan Club

25. **What does McCandless admit to having a fear of?**
   A. The dark
   B. Bears
   C. Water
   D. Moose

Quiz 2 Answer Key

1. **(D)** Emory
2. **(A)** Gaylord Stuckey
3. **(C)** Doctor Zhivago
4. **(C)** Sir John Franklin
5. **(C)** $25,000
6. **(C)** The boggy ground makes for very slow going
7. **(B)** Virginia
8. **(D)** Golf
9. **(C)** Canoeing
10. **(D)** Alaska
11. **(C)** Poisonous mold on potato seeds he ate
12. **(C)** An Italian restaurant
13. **(D)** Gordon Samel
14. **(D)** Carine
15. **(B)** Doing the jobs that no one else wanted
16. **(A)** John Waterman
17. **(C)** A cable running across the river
18. **(C)** Winnetka
19. **(D)** Ronald Franz
20. **(D)** He buries it unprotected
21. **(D)** Alaska
22. **(C)** Mistaking a caribou for a moose
23. **(C)** John Muir
24. **(B)** College Republican Club
25. **(C)** Water

Quiz 3

1. **Why doesn't McCandless get a hunting license?**
    A. He would have to use his real name to get one
    B. He canâ'Žt afford it
    C. He doesnâ'Žt have time before he starts his trek
    D. He doesnâ'Žt think itâ'Žs the governmentâ'Žs business to regulate
what he hunts and eats

2. **What is found written at the site of McCandless's death?**
    A. "I am Christopher McCandless"
    B. "I'm sorry"
    C. "Jack London is King"
    D. "I love Alaska"

3. **What happens to McCandless's Datsun after it is found?**
    A. Itâ'Žs returned to the manufacturer
    B. It is used for undercover agents doing drug deals
    C. Itâ'Žs junked
    D. Chrisâ'Žs parents take it back to Virginia

4. **Which of these is the most commonly held belief of what happened to Everett Ruess?**
    A. He lived the rest of his life in secret anonymity
    B. He was murdered
    C. He drowned
    D. He fell to his death while climbing on a canyon

5. **What sport is best for McCandless's personality?**
    A. Tennis
    B. Distance running
    C. Golf
    D. Racquet ball

6. **Where does McCandless get the sleeping bag that he dies in?**
    A. His mother sews it for him
    B. He makes it himself
    C. Jim Gallien gives it to him
    D. He finds it in the bus

7. **Why do the McCandlesses regret that Chris didn't take their dog, Buckley, with him when he left?**
    A. They think he couldâ'Žve sent Buckley for help
    B. They think he wouldâ'Žve had to come home when Buckley got a little bit older
    C. They think he wouldâ'Žve been more careful, less willing to risk Buckleyâ'Žs life than his own
    D. They wished Chris could have had Buckleyâ'Žs companionship when he was dying

8. **When does McCandless stop communicating with his parents?**
    A. After graduating from high school
    B. After graduating from Emory
    C. Right before going into the Alaska bush
    D. After almost drowning in Mexico

9. **Which of the following is the most likely reason Krakauer becomes obsessed with McCandless?**
    A. They are distantly related
    B. He sees a lot of parallels between McCandless and himself when he was younger
    C. They grew up in the same town and ran cross country together
    D. He has always been particularly obsessed with Alaska

10. **What is McCandless's maternal grandfather especially fond of?**
    A. Sports
    B. Animals
    C. Drinking
    D. Money

11. **What class does McCandless fail?**
    A. English
    B. Physics
    C. Gym
    D. Government

12. **What is the one thing Carine says she was better at than Chris?**
    A. Cross country
    B. Playing the French horn
    C. Making money
    D. Acting

13. **What is McCandless's safety net in Alaska?**
    A. A Parks Department cabin he knows is only a few miles away
    B. A radio he brings
    C. He doesn't have one
    D. He asks Jim Gallien to check up on him if he hasnâ'Žt heard from
    him in two months

14. **What does McCandless help Jan Burres do?**
    A. Sell books
    B. Hunt
    C. Teach people to live off the land
    D. Make leather belts

15. **Whose father ends up losing his mind?**
    A. Wayne Westberg
    B. Chris McCandless
    C. Carl McCunn
    D. Jon Krakauer

16. **What food does McCandless bring with him to Denali?**
    A. 40 granola bars
    B. A ten pound bag of rice
    C. Nothing
    D. Four packs of beef jersey

17. **What does the charity that McCandless donates his entire savings to
    do?**
    A. Promote literacy
    B. HIV and AIDS research
    C. Provide shelter to the homeless
    D. Fight hunger

18. **Where does McCandless stop for an unusually long time?**
    A. Bullhead City
    B. Las Vegas
    C. Carthage
    D. The Mojave Desert

19. **Which of these authors does McCandless especially love?**
    A. William Faulkner
    B. Jack London
    C. James Joyce
    D. Shakespeare

20. **Who of these people employs McCandless?**
    A. Everett Ruess
    B. Walt McCandless
    C. Wayne Westerberg
    D. Ronald Franz

21. **With whom is Chris's relationship most strained?**
    A. Walt McCandless
    B. Wayne Westerberg
    C. Billie McCandless
    D. Carine McCandless

22. **Which of the following does not describe McCandless?**
    A. Under prepared
    B. Suicidal
    C. Stubborn
    D. Naive

23. **Which of these characters' risky behavior is probably intentionally suicidal?**
    A. John Waterman
    B. Chris McCandless
    C. Carl McCunn
    D. Jon Krakauer

24. **Who is Wayne Westerberg?**
    A. The owner of a grain elevator who hires McCandless
    B. The private investigator Walt and Billie hire to find Chris
    C. A young mountain climber who becomes increasingly insane and obsessed with climbing
    D. An electrician who is the last person to see McCandless alive

25. **In what city does McCandless go to college?**
    A. Bullhead City
    B. Atlanta
    C. Fairbanks
    D. Miami

Quiz 3 Answer Key

1. **(D)** He doesn't think it's the government's business to regulate what he hunts and eats
2. **(C)** "Jack London is King"
3. **(B)** It is used for undercover agents doing drug deals
4. **(D)** He fell to his death while climbing on a canyon
5. **(B)** Distance running
6. **(A)** His mother sews it for him
7. **(C)** They think he would've been more careful, less willing to risk Buckley's life than his own
8. **(B)** After graduating from Emory
9. **(B)** He sees a lot of parallels between McCandless and himself when he was younger
10. **(B)** Animals
11. **(B)** Physics
12. **(B)** Playing the French horn
13. **(C)** He doesn't have one
14. **(A)** Sell books
15. **(D)** Jon Krakauer
16. **(B)** A ten pound bag of rice
17. **(D)** Fight hunger
18. **(A)** Bullhead City
19. **(B)** Jack London
20. **(C)** Wayne Westerberg
21. **(A)** Walt McCandless
22. **(B)** Suicidal
23. **(A)** John Waterman
24. **(A)** The owner of a grain elevator who hires McCandless
25. **(B)** Atlanta

Quiz 4

1. **Who of the following does McCandless stay in written contact with during his travels?**
   A. Jan Burres
   B. Carine McCandless
   C. Jim Gallien
   D. Jon Krakauer

2. **Which of the following does McCandless believe about hunting?**
   A. One should only eat meat if it is the only option besides starvation
   B. Only cruel people are capable of it
   C. It is immoral to waste any part of the animal that is killed
   D. One should only hunt male animals

3. **What is a rubber tramp?**
   A. A vagabond who doesnâ'Žt have a vehicle
   B. A tire salesman
   C. A sneaker salesman
   D. A vagabond who has a vehicle

4. **Which of the following does McCandless learn to make beautifully?**
   A. Leather belts
   B. Sleeping bags and quilts
   C. Totem poles
   D. Pipes

5. **Where does most of the information about McCandless's travels come from?**
   A. The memoir he was working on about his trip
   B. Police reports
   C. His photojournal
   D. His letters to Jan Burres and Wayne Westerberg

6. **Which of the following does McCandless not do in preparation for his Alaska trip?**
   A. Calisthenics
   B. Alert the park service to his plans
   C. Find out about preserving meat
   D. Learn about edible plants

7. **Which of the following is McCandless not accused of?**
   A. Starting a forest fire
   B. Having too much hubris
   C. Mistaking a caribou for a moose
   D. Vandalizing cabins in the area around the bus

8. **What makes McCandless very angry at his parents around the time of graduation?**
   A. Their refusal to let him live with them
   B. Their insistence he go to the graduation ceremonies
   C. Their offer to buy him a car
   D. Their insistence he go to medical school

9. **Who is Ronald Franz?**
   A. McCandlessâ'Žs maternal grandfather
   B. An elderly man who took a strong liking to McCandless
   C. McCandlessâ'Žs manager at the McDonaldâ'Žs in Bullhead City
   D. A British naval officer who led over one hundred men to their deaths

10. **Which of the following is not a problem McCandless has with his parents?**
    A. He feels betrayed that they lied to him about their past
    B. He thinks they try to control him too much
    C. He thinks they drink too much
    D. He thinks their wealth is immoral

11. **What high school team is McCandless captain of?**
    A. Soccer
    B. Tennis
    C. Cross Country
    D. Golf

12. **What climbing goal of Krakauer's does he compare to McCandless's Alaska trip?**
    A. The Devils Thumb
    B. Mt. Everest
    C. Mt. McKinley
    D. Davis Gulch

13. What happens to McCandless's Datsun?

A. It's stolen when he's camping

B. He abandons it after it gets flooded

C. He sells it for money for food

D. He gives it to another vagabond he meets

14. Who is Jim Gallien?

A. One of the hunters who find McCandless's body

B. An elderly man who took a strong liking to McCandless

C. A young mountain climber who becomes increasingly insane and obsessed with climbing

D. An electrician who is the last person to see McCandless alive

15. Which of the following does Krakauer not parallel to his own life?

A. McCandless's recklessness

B. McCandless's natural intelligence

C. McCandless's obsession with the wilderness

D. McCandless's troubled relationship with his father

16. Why does Carine think McCandless doesn't contact her after he leaves Atlanta?

A. He doesn't want to have any ties to his past

B. They've never been very close

C. He knows his parents will track him down if he does

D. He is disgusted with her materialism

17. What takes up most of McCandless's days in the Alaskan wilderness?

A. Rock climbing

B. Writing

C. Creating a map of the area

D. Tracking and hunting small game

18. What is Carl McCunn's fatal error?

A. Not arranging to be picked up at the end of his trip

B. Starting a fire too close to his camp

C. Mistaking poisoned plants for edible ones

D. Thinking there would be enough plants and fish so he wouldn't need to hunt

19. **For most of the two years leading to his Alaskan trip, where does McCandless usually say he is from?**
    A. Mexico
    B. Atlanta
    C. Virginia
    D. South Dakota

20. **What do McCandless's parents believe he is going to do after graduating Emory?**
    A. Go to law school
    B. Go to graduate school in Philosophy
    C. Work for OXFAM
    D. Go to medical school

21. **How does McCandless get to the sea in Mexico with a canoe?**
    A. He hitchhikes and then buys a canoe
    B. He canoes through canals leading to the sea
    C. He carries his canoe
    D. He and his canoe are towed by duck hunters

22. **What does McCandless not have a specific problem with?**
    A. Authority
    B. Alcoholism
    C. Dishonesty
    D. Materialism

23. **Why does McCandless spend time with Charlie even though he thinks he is crazy?**
    A. Charlie knows a lot about Alaska to tell McCandless
    B. McCandless wants to get to know all types of people
    C. There is no one else to help Charlie and McCandless wonâ'Žt desert him
    D. Charlie gives him a place to stay

24. **What do McCandless's coworkers at McDonald's have a problem with?**
    A. His rudeness to customers who are rude to him
    B. His hygiene
    C. His unreliability
    D. His drinking

25. **Which of the following damages McCandless's car?**
    A. Tornado
    B. Driving offroad
    C. Earthquake
    D. Flood

Quiz 4 Answer Key

1. (**A**) Jan Burres
2. (**C**) It is immoral to waste any part of the animal that is killed
3. (**D**) A vagabond who has a vehicle
4. (**A**) Leather belts
5. (**C**) His photojournal
6. (**B**) Alert the park service to his plans
7. (**A**) Starting a forest fire
8. (**C**) Their offer to buy him a car
9. (**B**) An elderly man who took a strong liking to McCandless
10. (**C**) He thinks they drink too much
11. (**C**) Cross Country
12. (**A**) The Devils Thumb
13. (**B**) He abandons it after it gets flooded
14. (**D**) An electrician who is the last person to see McCandless alive
15. (**B**) McCandless's natural intelligence
16. (**C**) He knows his parents will track him down if he does
17. (**D**) Tracking and hunting small game
18. (**A**) Not arranging to be picked up at the end of his trip
19. (**D**) South Dakota
20. (**A**) Go to law school
21. (**D**) He and his canoe are towed by duck hunters
22. (**B**) Alcoholism
23. (**D**) Charlie gives him a place to stay
24. (**B**) His hygiene
25. (**D**) Flood

ClassicNotes

Gr**A**deSaver™

Getting you the grade since 1999™

Other ClassicNotes from GradeSaver™

For our full list of over 250 Study Guides, Quizzes,
Sample College Application Essays, Literature Essays and E-texts, visit:

www.gradesaver.com

ClassicNotes

GrAdeSaver™

Getting you the grade since 1999™

Other ClassicNotes from GradeSaver™

I, Claudius
An Ideal Husband
Iliad
The Importance of Being
   Earnest
In Cold Blood
In Our Time
In the Time of the
   Butterflies
Inherit the Wind
An Inspector Calls
Interpreter of Maladies
Into the Wild
Invisible Man
The Island of Dr. Moreau
Jane Eyre
Jazz
The Jew of Malta
Joseph Andrews
The Joy Luck Club
Julius Caesar
The Jungle
Jungle of Cities
Kama Sutra
Kate Chopin's Short
   Stories
Kidnapped
King Lear
King Solomon's Mines
The Kite Runner
Last of the Mohicans
Leaves of Grass
The Legend of Sleepy
   Hollow
A Lesson Before Dying
Leviathan

Libation Bearers
Life is Beautiful
Life of Pi
Light In August
Like Water for Chocolate
The Lion, the Witch and
   the Wardrobe
Little Women
Lolita
Long Day's Journey Into
   Night
Look Back in Anger
Lord Jim
Lord of the Flies
The Lord of the Rings:
   The Fellowship of the
   Ring
The Lord of the Rings:
   The Return of the
   King
The Lord of the Rings:
   The Two Towers
A Lost Lady
The Lottery and Other
   Stories
Love in the Time of
   Cholera
The Love Song of J.
   Alfred Prufrock
The Lovely Bones
Lucy
Macbeth
Madame Bovary
Maggie: A Girl of the
   Streets and Other
   Stories

Manhattan Transfer
Mankind: Medieval
   Morality Plays
Mansfield Park
The Marrow of Tradition
The Master and
   Margarita
MAUS
The Mayor of
   Casterbridge
Measure for Measure
Medea
Merchant of Venice
Metamorphoses
The Metamorphosis
Middlemarch
A Midsummer Night's
   Dream
Moby Dick
A Modest Proposal and
   Other Satires
Moll Flanders
Mother Courage and Her
   Children
Mrs. Dalloway
Much Ado About
   Nothing
My Antonia
Mythology
The Namesake
Native Son
Nickel and Dimed: On
   (Not) Getting By in
   America
Night
Nine Stories

For our full list of over 250 Study Guides, Quizzes,
Sample College Application Essays, Literature Essays and E-texts, visit:

www.gradesaver.com

ClassicNotes

GradeSaver™

Getting you the grade since 1999™

Other ClassicNotes from GradeSaver™

Silas Marner
Sir Gawain and the
 Green Knight
Sister Carrie
Six Characters in Search
 of an Author
Slaughterhouse Five
Snow Falling on Cedars
The Social Contract
Something Wicked This
 Way Comes
Song of Roland
Song of Solomon
Songs of Innocence and
 of Experience
Sons and Lovers
The Sorrows of Young
 Werther
The Sound and the Fury
The Spanish Tragedy
Spenser's Amoretti and
 Epithalamion
Spring Awakening
The Stranger
A Streetcar Named
 Desire
Sula
The Sun Also Rises
Tale of Two Cities
The Taming of the Shrew
The Tempest
Tender is the Night
Tess of the D'Urbervilles
Their Eyes Were
 Watching God
Things Fall Apart

The Things They Carried
A Thousand Splendid
 Suns
The Threepenny Opera
Through the Looking
 Glass
Thus Spoke Zarathustra
The Time Machine
Titus Andronicus
To Build a Fire
To Kill a Mockingbird
To the Lighthouse
The Tortilla Curtain
Touching Spirit Bear
Treasure Island
Trifles
Troilus and Cressida
Tropic of Cancer
Tropic of Capricorn
Tuesdays With Morrie
The Turn of the Screw
Twelfth Night
Twilight
Ulysses
Uncle Tom's Cabin
Utopia
Vanity Fair
A Very Old Man With
 Enormous Wings
Villette
The Visit
Volpone
Waiting for Godot
Waiting for Lefty
Walden
Washington Square

The Waste Land
The Wealth of Nations
Where the Red Fern
 Grows
White Fang
A White Heron and
 Other Stories
White Noise
White Teeth
Who's Afraid of Virginia
 Woolf
Wide Sargasso Sea
Wieland
Winesburg, Ohio
The Winter's Tale
The Woman Warrior
Wordsworth's Poetical
 Works
Woyzeck
A Wrinkle in Time
Wuthering Heights
The Yellow Wallpaper
Yonnondio: From the
 Thirties
Zeitoun

For our full list of over 250 Study Guides, Quizzes,
Sample College Application Essays, Literature Essays and E-texts, visit:

www.gradesaver.com

91579684R00061

Made in the USA
Lexington, KY
23 June 2018